Le Chat Noir EXPOSED

*The Absurdist Spirit Behind
a 19th Century French Cabaret*

Caroline Crépiat

TRANSLATED FROM THE FRENCH BY DOUG SKINNER

BLACK SCAT BOOKS
2021

LE CHAT NOIR EXPOSED
The Absurdist Spirit Behind a 19th Century French Cabaret
by Caroline Crépiat

ISBN-13 978-1-7356159-6-7

Front cover: Eugène Samuel Grasset, watercolor study for the *Le Théâtre du Chat Noir* (1886). Cover & book design: N. Conquest

ACKNOWLEDGMENTS

Please note, since this page cannot legibly accommodate all the notices, page 180 constitutes an extension of this copyright page. The publisher wishes to express gratitude for the kind permission to translate and publish these articles, which originally appeared in the following publications in France:

"Les logiques de connexions au *Chat Noir*" appeared in *Logiques et dynamiques des groupes littéraires*, Denis Saint-Amand (ed.), Liège, Presses Universitaires de Liège (2016).

"Donner sa langue aux lecteurs du *Chat Noir*" appeared in *Les voix du lecteur dans la presse française au XIX⸱ siècle*, Elina Absalyamova, Valérie Stiénon (ed.), Limoges, Presses Universitaires de Limoges (2018).

"Le fumisme n'est pas qu'une affaire d'hommes – Le fumisme dans les poèmes des femmes du *Chat Noir* ou l'ambivalence d'une énonciation de l'altérité " appeared in *Poésie au féminin*, Patricia Godi-Tkatchouk (ed.) (2011), to be published again in *Poésie au féminin/Poétique(s) du corps*, Patricia Godi-Tkatchouk, Lucie Lavergne (ed.), Revue *Résonances* (2021).

BLACK SCAT BOOKS
Publishers of Sublime Art & Literature
BlackScatBooks.com

CONTENTS

⚘INTRODUCTION⚘

L e *Chat Noir* is known universally by a promotional image produced quite late in its history: the poster for the eponymous cabaret's touring company, created by Steinlen in 1896, showing a black cat on a yellow background, its head flanked by a red halo evoking a stained-glass window, bearing the inscription "Montjoye Montmartre." Judging by this cat, sanctified, sitting in majesty, the Montmartre cabaret is then at the height of its glory; its name is on everyone's lips, the public flocks to its evening performances, which combine songs, poetry, and especially shadow puppet plays, created by Henri Rivière, and which made *Le Chat Noir* truly a place of entertainment appreciated throughout Paris. The cabaret itself had, besides, become an obligatory and picturesque place, due to the numerous paintings and illustrations by the artists who frequented it—Willette, Jules Chéret, Antonio de La Gandara, and especially Steinlen— that adorn the walls, and the numerous curiosities that decorate it—the skull of Louis XIII as a child being a favorite example—but also due to the welcome given its customers: the waiters dressed as academicians, and the slang, archaisms, and quips of the *gentilhomme-cabaretier*, Rodolphe Salis.

However, the activities organized under this emblem are even more diversified. In particular, there is an eponymous paper, which appears weekly from January 14, 1882 to September 4, 1897, produced mostly by the artists who frequent the cabaret. This corpus, quite vast (780 issues), is the principal material on which our study is based, inasmuch as it lets us read the grievances, stakes, and strategies that drive the group, and lets us determine, in a more literary and artistic fashion, the specific aesthetic it elaborates. Even more, the paper *Le Chat Noir* is crucial in helping us to identify the emergence and consecration of such a group, and especially the components of that distinctive spirit, *fumisme*, on which it is based.

In fact, in the beginning, there was another paper, *L'Hydropathe*, first issued in January 1879 and lasting until May 1880, produced by a group of young artists, poets, and musicians who met in a room in the Latin Quarter under the name of the *Club des Hydropathes*. Founded at the end of 1878 by Émile Goudeau, poet and journalist, it included those who were to participate in the first Chat Noir: Maurice Rollinat, Marie Krysinska, Charles Cros, Georges Lorin, André Gill, Sapeck, Jules Jouy, and Alphonse

Allais, to name only a few. It is within this group—capricious, bohemian, subversive, childish, and already *fumiste*—that they first recite and sing their own works on stage.[1] Two years later, we find Émile Goudeau as editor-in-chief of the paper *Le Chat Noir*.[2] In fact, after his decisive meeting in 1881 with Rodolphe Salis, who was a mediocre painter, but had just opened a bar, at 84 boulevard Rochechouart, Montmartre, which he hoped to give some artistic character, Goudeau sees a way to revive his editorial and artistic activities with the *Hydropathes*, and perhaps find a new audience by moving his group from the Latin Quarter. At his instigation, *Le Chat Noir* becomes, from its opening in 1881, the new home of the *Hydropathes*. As Raymond de Casteras emphasizes, "*Hydropathes*, Hirsutes,[3] and *Chat Noir* were simply successive names for the same migratory troupe, which changed its label when it changed its premises."[4] The *Chat Noir* cabaret inherits this whole little world, and everything they had tried out in their eponymous club. Salis, who recognizes in these artistic gatherings a way to turn a profit, in order to promote them, founds with Émile Goudeau the paper, an "organ of the interests of Montmartre" and of those of the cabaret. So, in the first issue, Salis proclaims his ambitions, in an illustration entitled "Our Program":[5] "Hold still! Everyone will pass!" cries an enormous black cat, ready to photograph all who pass before it. A double program in reality: no one will escape the critical and subversive gaze of *Le Chat Noir*, and no one will resist the appeal of the cabaret.

In concrete terms, *Le Chat Noir* is published in the form of a newspaper, 30 by 40 centimeters, four pages, from 1882 to 1895: the format is changed at the launch of the new series, reduced to 20 by 26 centimeters, and comprising eight pages from then on, on the model of other papers like *Le Rire*, which had debuted the previous year. A weekly, it is produced autonomously by the producer itself—the cabaret—which also distributes it at first, that is, from hand to hand, for a low price, or even passed out free to the students and bohemians who form its boisterous clientele in the beginning. Later, it is sold by kiosks or street vendors: subscriptions are also offered from the first issue, for six months or a year, both in Paris and the provinces. A none too opulent paper, printed in black and white, its circulation never ceases to grow, reaching 20,000 copies in its hours of glory. It is dedicated to producing humorous texts and cartoons, and Goudeau's editorials follow the same satirical bent, mocking all the faults of contemporary society, from politics to the fields of media, literature, and art. Although its columns are not, strictly speaking, divided into sections, it follows an order that rarely changes. The cover illustration and a political or literary editorial ("Bulletin") by Goudeau, replaced after several years by a humorous story from George Auriol or Alphonse Allais, take up the first page; the second page is devoted to texts—poems or stories; an illustration—either a large drawing or a picture story with or without words—occupies the third page; less often, there are poems with borders or illustrated songs with music;[6] the last page, finally, is dedicated to reports of recent works, reviews of shows, and ads.

Although, at first, the paper is used by the cabaret to promote itself, notably by publishing the texts recited and the songs sung in chorus there, it soon surpasses that simple function and aims for a larger and larger audience. At the same time, the cabaret is attracting such crowds that Rodolphe Salis is obliged, in 1885, to move it from its original small space into a townhouse, at 12 rue de Laval, Montmartre. Not all the original artists follow him: rebaptized the *Hostellerie du Chat Noir* [Black Cat Inn], it becomes a fashionable and lucrative place, which some find too commercial. The larger space permits the launching of an innovative supplementary activity, which in fact will eventually supersede the readings, then relegated to interludes: the shadow puppet theater created by Henri Rivière. Let us cite some of the plays performed there: *L'Épopée* [*The Epic*] (1887), by Caran d'Ache, with music by Charles de Sivry, Albert Tinchant, and Claude Debussy; *La Marche à l'étoile* [*The Walk to the Star*] (1890), with text and music by Georges Fragerolle; and *Ailleurs!* [*Elsewhere!*] (1891), a play by Maurice Donnay, set to music by Charles de Sivry. After having won his gamble to turn Montmartre into the center of the world, flipping it from dominated to dominant, Salis sets out to conquer France with a new activity superimposed on the others: the *Chat Noir* tours, from 1892 to 1897. It is during one of these that he falls ill, only to die a few days later, on March 19, 1897. The cabaret closes in January, and the paper continues until September. On the social and cultural horizon of its age, *Le Chat Noir*, with all of its various activities, plays the role of innovator: whether it be in the pleasures and shows of the previously marginal neighborhood of Montmartre, in fashions, such as the turn-of-the-century monologue created by Charles Cros with Coquelin Cadet, or in the replacement of the elite, whether intellectual, political, or societal, by the ebullient activity of bohemian artists, some of whom, accordingly, become celebrities themselves. Already widely imitated at the time—notably by *Le Mirliton* [*The Kazoo*], the cabaret and paper directed by Aristide Bruant[7] (1887-1895), *L'Âne Rouge* [*The Red Ass*], the cabaret founded by the brother—and rival—of Salis (1889-1905), or *L'Hostellerie du Lyon d'Or* [The Golden Lion Inn] of François Trombert[8] (1891-1893)—*Le Chat Noir* seems never to have been equalled. Just as "*Le Chat*—as a flame attracts a moth—called to itself musicians, sculptors, painter, and poets,"[9] this entity with its multiple talents distilled and, even more, incarnated the spirit of a time and place, Montmartre, still marked by the Commune and the repression that followed: a free, independent, joyful, noisy spirit, hungry for collective and popular celebrations, both day and night.

The numerous activities of *Le Chat Noir* are reflected in the paper: the key words, in effect, are variegation and eclecticism. *Le Chat Noir* has this in particular, that it adheres to no school, to no precise movement. There are accordingly diverse, even divergent, esthetics in different genres— poets are joined by singers, like Jules Jouy and Aristide Bruant—in varying arts—composers like Charles Sivry and Marcel Legay, cartoonists including Willette, Steinlen, and Caran d'Ache, and humorists like Alphonse Allais and George Auriol; many men, but also a few women, such as Marie Krysinska. The artists, besides, often have several talents that they exercise equally. For example: Charles de Sivry can play piano for the shadow puppet plays in the cabaret[10] as well as publish fantastic tales in the paper;[11] certain poets assume the role of fanciful reporters, such as Émile Goudeau, under the pseudonym of A'Kempis, making "Voyages of Discovery"[12] into the distant lands of Paris; in 1884, Jules Jouy organizes contests for readers, under the title of "Weekly Puzzle"; Rodolphe Salis himself, besides tending bar, greeting his clients with invective and truculent remarks, and introducing the next artist to take the stage, illustrates the paper in the beginning, and publishes bawdy tales in mock archaic French.[13] Added to that is an absence of hierarchy: for example, marginal poets like Eugène Godin or Georges Camuset see themselves published next to poets who are already famous, like Mallarmé or Verlaine. We shall not cite all the collaborators in this presentation: simply mentioning the name of Léon Bloy, who offers virulent commentary on the literature of the time (1883-1884) beside those of Adolphe Willette, bohemian painter and illustrator, who revives the character of Pierrot; Jules Jouy, anarchist singer; Marie Krysinska, who later mounts a bitter campaign to claim the maternity of free verse; Willy, facetious society critic and hoaxer; Maurice Donnay, playwright and poet, future Academician; Charles Cros, poet, former Zutiste, inventor of the phonograph and the *fumiste* monologue; or other young artists, like Paul Adam, Jean Lorrain, and Francis Jammes, whose first texts are published there, gives a hint of the joyful jumble of personalities and esthetics we are about to enter.

Despite these disparities, one founding principle seems to preside over the esthetic cohesion of the group: *fumisme*.[14] Georges Fragerolle is the first, in *L'Hydropathe*,[15] to try to define *fumisme*, and more particularly the man who practices it, the *fumiste*, and to that end contrasts him with the "man of wit":

"Under an outer layer that is almost pompous, and therefore naive, he hides the core of skepticism that is the very stuff of wit. To make someone feel, in a large group, by a series of words, that he is an imbecile, is the nature of wit. To agree with him and hand him the very quintessence of his imbecility, is the nature of *fumisme*. Wit asks to be paid at once with bravos and discreet smiles, *fumisme* carries within itself its own reward: it is art for art's sake. To pass for a man of wit, it is sometimes enough to be an ass in a lion's skin: to be a good *fumiste*, it is often indispensable to be a lion in an ass's skin. In the first case, the effect is direct, in the second, it is reflected once, twice, often ten times."

The point is clear: *fumisme* is a modern—state-of-the-art—form of humor. It aims to make a mockery, systematically, of all serious discourse—conceived as a product of the pervading solemnity—and its ensuing codes, like common sense and the proper usage of common terms, all while staying serious. Think of Alphonse Allais who, when he told one of his funny stories "to double over"[16] a few friends at a cafe table, always kept a straight face. There is also Maurice Mac-Nab, who, reading one of his great successes, "La Ballade des Foetus" [The Ballad of the Fetuses], made the audience "laugh to tears"[17] when he recited it "in his impassive wooden voice."[18] *Fumisme* is above all a posture, paradoxical, which disconcerts us with its complexity, and qualifies the laughter that is traditionally expected. The author gets laughs from what does not usually get laughs (fetuses, for example). First of all, because to be a *fumiste* comes back to presenting oneself in disguise. Fragerolle himself plays with a certain trompe l'oeil in his resemanticization of characters in fairy tales and fables who use animal skins to trick other characters, like *Peau d'Âne* [Donkey Skin], the princess who wore a donkey skin to avoid recognition, or the wolf wrapped in a goatskin to trick the kid and show him his "white paw,"[19] and by redoubling them: in truth, the *fumiste*'s ultimate ruse derives from wearing a mask beneath the mask. The mask is what is exhibited, but is used not to hide, but to show something else, which remains no less enigmatic. For, second modality of *fumisme*, its mechanisms are complex, and above all unexpected: the indistinct form of an "art for art's sake" of absurd logic, a gratuitous laugh in action, it consists of a discourse that is always indirect ("reflective"), in a systematic distancing. As Fragerolle emphasizes, the goal is not to get a laugh at any cost. On the contrary, if laughter comes, it is because the reader or spectator is tricked, his expectations deceived: his laughter is forced, because, as Daniel Grojnowski and Bernard Sarrazin emphasize, *fumisme* "places the receiver—like the producer—in a position of unstable equilibrium that brings unease to the intellect [...] and the somewhat sophisticated pleasure of escaping the constraints of the senses, the pleasure of the undecidable."[20]

For a better definition of this "undecidable" aspect, this generalized thumbing of the nose at the reader or spectator, this disordering of everything, which borders on the famous "derangement of all the senses" from the turn of the century, but permits no epiphany, we must turn to another attempt at definition, this time by Émile Goudeau. In his memoirs, written when he was still in the prime of life (39), *Dix ans de bohème* [*Ten Years of Bohemia*], he proposes several formulas: "a sort of disdain for everything, a contempt inside for all beings and all things, which translates on the outside into innumerable attacks, jokes, and hoaxes,"[21] "a kind of internal madness, translated on the outside into imperturbable buffooneries."[22] *Fumisme* then would be a skewed, discordant, and ephemeral translation of an internal state, which by an assortment of techniques, would condemn all representation (of oneself, of the world) to self-nullification. Let us remember that at the time, the fashion was for Decadence, for unhealthy states of languor, for neurosis. The Decadent distinguishes himself from the rest of society by a haughty pose ("disdain"), by the outdated ennui he carries with him, by a delicate fervor stamped with mysticism for everything he finds rare, curious, or artificial. To hear this "disdain" then commonly shared by artists and writers at the turn of the century provoke disparate uncontrollable laughter shows how subversive the *fumiste* position is. It is a question of freeing oneself from all norms, even the most avant-gardist, even the most transgressive. The very dynamism of the *fumiste*—and *chatnoiresque*—discourse, mixing the solemn with the light, the insignificant with the mirific, never ceases to make the claim that everything serious—whether worldly, social, or political—is a fraud, and to lay bare all the ensuing results and conventions—the better to distinguish oneself from it. Even if it means raising a common banner, which, in essence, is itself only one more mystification. And yet, as we shall see throughout the course of this work, *fumisme*, by the sacrilege it commits against art and literature, among other things, has been able to reinvent the mechanisms of discourse, to display its artifices and deficiencies, to refine the absurd by not relying on the ludic techniques used everywhere else, and to give, finally, that specific coloration to the texts published, spoken, performed, and sung at *Le Chat Noir*.

This work gathers together ten articles published in various collective works, some of them especially rewritten. It proposes an exploration of this social space that left its mark on our cultural and artistic history, by passing in review, in broad strokes, the essential themes and problems addressed in its associated paper, without, however, neglecting to reveal fully the polyphonic aspect of the group, incorporating. for example, the gendered perception of *fumisme*. The aim is to bring to light the constituent elements of a genuine esthetic, disguised as a joke, of anti-bourgeois provocation or of anti-romantico-symbolisto-decadent expression.

If the reputation—and legend!—of *Le Chat Noir* precedes it as an essential place of entertainment at the end of the 19th century, and if we can now give a name to the very specific form of humor the group brandished as a standard, what did they laugh at in *Le Chat Noir*? This is what the reading of *Le Chat Noir Exposed* is about to reveal to you.

PART 1:

A POLYPHONIC GROUPISM

CHAPTER ONE
Group Logic

The staff of *Le Chat Noir*, before the shadow puppet theater, *Le Figaro Illustré*, June 1896.

"The *Chat Noir* cabaret is the most Astonishing, Marvelous, Bizarre, Grandiose, Stupefying, Vibrant Creation in all of the centuries felled by the Scythe of Time." Right away, with this announcement inserted in the paper at its beginnings—from 1882 to 1885—the tone is given: the *Chat Noir* proclaims itself as superlatively unique. Whereas in the *Hydropathes*—who prefigure the *Chat Noir*—it was a question of promoting each of the individuals comprising the group,[1] the *chatnoiresque* strategy, more agressive and expansive, akin to propaganda, puts forth a community that unceasingly represents itself. And yet this community is not a given: the artists come from all geographical, as well as esthetic, horizons; furthermore, the permanent recombination of the group might explain the long life of both the cabaret and its paper. It is a matter of organizing a group cohesion, of fabricating it, first to launch the cabaret, and second, to sustain it.

How do these connections play out? If we can establish a certain number of them, they reveal themselves as fully protean as the group itself, all constantly challenged and reformulated. It is in terms of its movements that we propose to examine this group effect: according to a centripetal movement at first, by the formulation of an exclusive lyrical subject, and, more broadly, of a society centered on itself, and then according to a more contrasting and sinuous movement, similar to the *fumiste* esthetic.

An Exclusive Lyric Subject

In this collective context, it is a question of setting the community onto a literary stage. This is particularly evident in the poetry of the *Chat Noir*, notably by means of the lyrical subject, which appears stretched, expanded, remodeled, and readapted to the image of the *Chat Noir* and to its group logic: the first person plural is preferred. If extending the subject beyond individuality is nothing new—Romantic poets in particular give the lyrical "I" a universal dimension, encompassing the one and the all— the poets of the *Chat Noir* attempt to give it a unifying aspect:

Oh! Soyons intenses!
Abusons des danses!
Abusons des lits
Et des seins polis!

[…]
Vivons d'oeuvres folles!
Disons des paroles
Qu'emporte le vent.[2]

[Oh! Let us be intense!
Let us overuse dances!
Let us overuse beds
And polished breasts!

[…]
Let us live by mad works!
Let us say words
Carried off by the wind.]

We therefore find again the ambiance of the cabaret, where the refrains of songs are taken up in chorus, like the "Chanson des Hydropathes"[3] by Charles Cros: "Hydropathes, chantons en choeur / La noble chanson des liqueurs!" [Hydropathes, let us sing in chorus / The noble song of liquors!]. All of the voices enter into communion, becoming one:

Pour oublier la vie et ses
Leurres, les plumes que nous prîmes
Exerçons-les en des essais
Ou s'entrelacent nos rimes;
[…]
Lyrique et funambule ami,
Accordons-nous: ut, sol, la, mi.[4]

[To forget life and its
Delusions, the quills that we took,

17

Let us exercise them in efforts
Where our rhymes interlace;
[…]
Lyric and funambulist friend,
Let us tune up: do, so, la, mi.]

The boundaries between "me" and "all" therefore appear abolished. The metaphor of a single body is furthermore spun out copiously, as in the "Ballade des Assassins," by means of the syntagma "Our hand": "Guenipes aux regards malsains, / […] Souffrez que notre main caresse / La gélatine de vos seins."[5] [Trollops with unhealthy looks, / […] Suffer our hand to caress / The gelatin of your breasts.]

Moved by the same *credo*, the subject does more than recognize himself in another that resembles him: otherness seems rejected in favor of the search for a collective and exclusive singularity. Paul Dollfus, in "Le Boulevard,"[6] therefore waxes ironic about the poetic ideal and the exclusion of the other, by boastfulness, hypocrisy, or the effect of a group like that at the *Chat Noir*:

«Je» est la personne qui parle.
«Tu», celle à qui l'on parle.
«Ils» ou «Elle» celle qui n'est pas là.

Conjugaison du Verbe «Avoir du Génie»
Indicatif présent

J'ai du génie.
Tu as du génie.
Il ou Elle n'a pas de génie.
Nous avons du génie.
Vous avez du génie.
Ils ou Elles n'ont pas de génie.

["I" is the person who speaks.
"You," the one to whom one speaks.
"He" or "She," the one who is not there.

Conjugation of the verb "To Have Genius"
Present indicative

I have genius.
You have genius.
He or She does not have genius.
We have genius.
You have genius.
They do not have genius.]

Symmetrically with this expansion of the subject's identity occurs that of the traditional lyrical address "you," not from the singular to the plural, but included in a specular dialogue: the lyrical statement is made in a group, crystallized in a fraternal consensus against a "them," the bourgeois, the great poet, or the authors then in fashion. The paper, like the cabaret, establishes itself as an autonomous cadre, a "world of its own";[7] the autonomy of the literary field is determined by the fact that the artist's audience consists of the other artists in the room. The intent of using the lyrical subject is then modified: personal emotion or amorous seduction is overturned in a *captatio benevolentiae*, which furthermore depends on allusions that only the members can understand at their true value. By this means, the apparent meaning of the text is also made autonomous, in an esthetic experience that is self-sufficient, by definition pragmatic, which takes place during the event, in accordance with the cadre of the cabaret.

It is not, in spite of everything, a question of effacing one's singularity as a poet or artist: the aim is to preserve the diversity of the group's members within a certain unity. Not resolving their contradictions maintains competition between artists, and keeps the group effervescent.

To stabilize to some extent this cohesion, it must be given some coherence, by turning to a singular ready-made common denominator: *Le Chat Noir*.

A "closed society"?[8]

It is around the motif of the black cat in particular—the animal, a symbol of liberty and bohemia, as much as the eponymous cabaret—that the bond of sociability crystallizes: the spatial bond changes into a symbolic bond that punctuates and reactualizes membership in the group, and whose spirit could be found nowhere else. Presented on the page by means of little black cats, the texts and illustrations are formed around this central figure. One could cite Steinlen's wordless picture stories, for example "Horrible fin d'un poisson rouge"[9] [Horrible end of a goldfish], or a story by Salis, "Le Chat de tante Agathe"[10] [Aunt Agatha's Pussy], with that equivocal meaning that artists never find tiresome. Pseudonyms also form part of this self-referential game: Constant Chanouard, Beauminet [Pretty Kitty], Miahou, or even Greffier [Mouser].

If it is a question of reappropriating the language and codes of the dominant society, the simple annexation of this paradigm seems to suffice. Thus, an alternative society is put in place, provided with a "Marseillaise des chats noirs"[11] and a "Faculté des sciences du *Chat Noir*."[12] Economic jargon is also reinvested and reduced to the scale of Matou, an alley cat, who writes the "Miaulements financiers"[13] [Financial Mewings]. Particular poetic genres also seem to be created on the same principle, like the "Sonnet-Montmartre"[14] by Raymondo de la Cazba, which fits a traditional form to the geographical situation of the place of creation. Although imbued with the picturesque qualities of Montmartre neighborhoods, and celebrating its emblematic places, like the Moulin de la Galette or the Sacré-Coeur, the "Sonnet-Montmartre" is no different than the parodistic sonnets written by the poets of *Le Chat Noir*. Its specificity is fabricated, depending solely on its title, and tends to return to the promotional logic of the cabaret, and of Montmartre.

If the singularity of *Le Chat Noir* is apparently not questioned, even today, it is the result, however, of fabulation, and of recurrent and exaggerated mythification. The distribution of the *chatnoiresque* motif, both in terms of the stated and the statement, seeks to recreate the world in its own image, paradoxically inscribing the group in something much larger. Jules Jouy exaggerates the point in this way by comparing the night to a black cat: "The night is nothing but a black cat, of such dimensions that it blots out the sun, and men can see only one of its eyes: the moon."[15] The concerted and imaginary reconstruction of a legendary past serves to legitimize the group and its cohesion—which is not without parodying the ancient method of the legitimization of power at the heart of la Cité by means of myth[16] — around a center that in fact would not be new, but would have always been "the center of the world."[17]

"It is high time to rectify an error that has weighed upon more than sixty complete generations. The Scripture that is called Holy—I'm not quite sure why—has only, to put it politely, mocked the people. […] We read in Genesis that Noah's ark anchored on *Mont Ararat*. What can *Mont Ararat* mean? Read: Montmartre! Indeed, that old drunkard Noah, when the diluvian waters began to recede, spied a mountaintop, and said, '*Je m'arrête*': 'I stop.' He must have been blind like Homer or one-eyed like Gambetta […] not to see that those two words, *Mont-m'arrête*, are the ineluctable roots of Montmartre. Therefore, Montmartre is the cradle of humanity."[18]

And when, in the spring of 1885, *Le Chat Noir* moves, leaving its cramped premises for an opulent townhouse of three stories, on the rue de Laval, it responds to its detractors with a stylistic pirouette, evoking a fairytale:

"And now disproportionately The Cat began to grow.
And It was gigantic.
And now Its pale green eyes, shining more and more, glittered like two stars.
[…] And The Cat still kept growing. And always more luminous Its eyes, and more teeming, in Its shadow, the admiring multitudes of men."[19]

The centripetal nature of the *Chat Noir* group, founded on "complicity and overstatement,"[20] seems, with time, following the example of that "Cat" of "disproportionate" dimensions, to enlarge its trajectory, to the point of attracting to itself quasi-universality.

But to play at claiming totalizing recognition does not eliminate its demands of declassification and decentralization. If it postulates a fraternal, even familial, bond—the artists invent an "uncle" in Francisque Sarcey and others,[21] the cabaret is their house[22] —it functions outside all obligatory or pre-established filiation. They thus blithely take up Paul Verlaine and Edmond Lepelletier's parody of a dedicatory letter by Victor Hugo for the collection *Poèmes saturniens*,[23] which stigmatized this cordial fraternity of peers as a bit conventional: "Colleague, for you are my colleague, in colleague [*confrère*] there is brother [*frère*]."[24] A picture story by Willette,[25] for example, shows Hugo, made up as a June bug, within a phrase tinged with ribaldry: "For, he murmured, in *confrère*, there is brother and sister!" (*con* meaning "cunt"). Without a compulsory patriarch, bonds are formed horizontally, on the same plane, as if the black cat's dietary beliefs become as crucial to the cohesion of the group as each member's poetic ambitions.

If one "seeks his fortune / Around the *Chat Noir*,"[26] and if turning, if not in a circle, at least idly, is a fantasy highly prized by these artists,[27] the system, which seems centripetal, is neither fixed nor rigid. The shared mask of this great Black Cat is nourished by the variable, sinuous, and even unexpected movements of the dialogic relations between the artists.

A Sinuous and Unexpected Dialogism

As in every group, collaboration is constant at the *Chat Noir*. Creations are made on several themes, or on the same one: one artist's text is illustrated[28] or set to music, or both at once,[29] by another; and inversely: one artist's wordless picture story is translated into a text by another.[30] *Le Livre d'or du Chat Noir* [*The Golden Book of the* Chat Noir], which Rodolphe Salis, the *gentilhomme-cabaretier*, left available at the entrance of the cabaret, also bears witness to this participatory writing. Adolphe Vautier wrote two quatrains in it, noting at the end what seems both a reminder for himself and a call for contribution: "(Demi-sonnet) / To be continued and improved,"[31] even if his signature directly beneath it might indicate, in spite of everything, that he's thumbing his nose at the practice.

The fashion is for circulation and for dialogism of ideas and ways of writing, but the associations are not lasting: all is in the movement. The collective experiments are organized around the mechanism of variation, and can appear on the same page[32] or spread across several issues. The game sometimes takes place across several years, such as, for example, a wordless picture story by Steinlen, "Le plus vexé des trois"[33] [The most upset of the three], showing a black cat and a white cat fighting over a little boy's bread and butter, which is reworked into a drawing by Heidbrinck, "Le moins heureux des trois"[34] [The unhappiest of the three], in which the pair of boy and bread is changed into a real couple, and the disturbing element becomes a drunk policeman; Léon Sandis,[35] finally, almost plagiarizes the first story, with the slight change of making one of the cats a dog. Often, a dialogue is established around the variation, such as "Spiritualisme"[36] by Armand Masson, which responds to "Philosophie—Sonnet honteux"[37] [Philosophy—Shameful Sonnet] by Edmond Haraucourt, by presenting it in reverse, while preserving its scatologico-religious character: if in Haraucourt, "God makes man," in the literal sense, and uses the occasion to sound his "intestinal organ," in Masson, "the soul of beans" escaping the human intestines, "s'envole vers les cieux, // Et […] / Charme de son parfum vague et délicieux / Le nez de Dieu pour qui les âmes sont égales." [flies up to heaven, // And […] / Charms with its vague and delicious perfume / the nose of God, for whom souls are equal.]

Furthermore, the parodies intertwine. So, one parodies one another within the group. For example, Djinn takes a malicious delight in imitating two series by Henry Somm, his "Pointes sèches"[38] [Drypoints] and his "Contes pour rendre les petits enfants fous"[39] [Tales to drive little children mad], by subverting the principle of the dedication: "Pointe sèche—pour embêter Somm"[40] [Drypoint—to irritate Somm] and "Conte polychrome—pour rendre fous les petits enfants de Somm"[41] [Polychromatic tale—to drive Somm's little children mad]. But the parodies are also, obviously, those of texts known to all, but whose main objective is changed into a ritual joke. In this way, "Le Vase brisé"[42] [The Broken Vase] by Sully Prudhomme, in particular its last verse, "Il est brisé, n'y touchez pas" [It is broken, do not touch it], held up to ridicule. Fred, in "Le Gosse frisé"[43] [The Curly-headed Child], subverts the *fissure* (crack) in the initial vase into a *frisure* (curling) that is just as unfortunate, and the sorrow of love into a child's tantrum:

> Il ne peut souffrir qu'on l'effleure,
> Et quand on le caresse, il pleure…
> *Il est frisé: n'y touchez pas!*

> [He cannot suffer anyone to touch him,
> And when caressed, he weeps…
> *He is curly-headed: don't touch him!*]

"Le «*pneu*» crevé"[44] [The Burst Tire] by Alfred Béjot reworks in its own way the idea of an object that breaks, or, rather, deflates:

> Le «*pneu*» de cette bicyclette
> Par un caillou fut éraflé.
> (Le *recordman* à l'aveuglette
> Avait, ce jour-là, pédalé.)

> Et la légère meurtrissure
> Dans le fragile caoutchouc,
> D'une marche invisible et sûre,
> A creusé lentement un trou.

> Son air comprimé sur la route
> Petit à petit s'est sauvé;
> Le «*pneu*» n'ira plus loin sans doute…
> N'y touchez pas, il est crevé!

> [The tire of this bicycle
> Was scratched by a pebble.
> (The record holder, that day,
> Had pedaled blindly.)

> And the slight bruise
> In the fragile rubber,
> By invisible and certain progress,
> Slowly opened a hole.

The compressed air, on the road,
Escaped bit by bit;
No doubt the tire will go no further…
Do not touch it, it has burst!]

Not only is it a question of parodying a great poet, who furthermore has the bad taste to be a Parnassian, but from parody to parody, there spring the poetics of the *Chat Noir*. Indeed, this story of the burst tire is an allegorization of a joke, in both the literal and figurative sense, that is exhausted to the maximum. It also echoes the *fumiste* esthetic, and its inflated texts that end by provoking bursts of laughter. This process of reworking furthermore leads to the evocation of one of the *Chat Noir*'s first artists, André Gill. In "Les poètes, boulevard Rochechouart"[45] by Jean Greffier, an imaginary conversation takes place between poets, such as Racine, Boileau, and Gautier. Sully Prudhomme is also in the group, and exclaims when talking about André Gill; "N'y touchez pas, il est fêlé!" [Don't touch him, he's cracked!]. The intertextual game moves toward a knowing wink between the poets familiar with Gill and his madness. By means of these games, the *fumiste* esthetic is formulated. Georges Fragerolle defines this in effect as speech that is always indirect, and even "reflected once, twice, often ten times."[46] Here, the parody really only takes effect later, in an "unexpected"[47] way. It happens as if bouncing from number to number, like the fin-de-siècle avatar of a fanciful Romantic *Zigzag*. Connections between artists are thus made in the collective pleasure of exploring this "reflected" movement, which plays out in the openings in the text to make the resonances between words, things, and individuals better understood.

These "reflected" effects proliferate, and open into a sort of collective "work in progress," leading artists to let other artists' esthetics into their own. Let us recall the first verses of the "Hareng saur"[48] [Salt Herring] by Charles Cros:

Il était un grand mur blanc—nu, nu, nu
Contre le mur, une échelle—haute, haute, haute,
Et par terre un hareng saur—sec, sec, sec.

[There was a big white wall—blank, blank, blank
Against the wall, a ladder—high, high, high,
And on the ground a salt herring—dry, dry, dry.]

The final vignette in a drawing by Willette, "L'Éléphant à trompe"[49] [The

25

Elephant with Trunk], reworks this poem, and emphasizes its nonsensical character by an unexpected collusion between an elephant and a spider. A hammer in its trunk, an elephant nails a salt herring to a blank wall. Rather than climbing a ladder set against the wall, the elephant stands on a hanging spiderweb, while the spider is spinning it. The elephant replaces, for the space of one "wordless story," the black cat, often the principal character in Willette's work. There is therefore a double dialogism here: Willette reworks at the same time the fanciful text of one of his comrades, and his own style by modifying it.[50]

The sinuous movements of this dialogism between artists of the *Chat Noir* can also take on the appearance of entanglements that can be somewhat paradoxical, even ironic. In effect, all strategies are valid to proclaim the cohesion of a "unique" group, and above all, a certain line of conduct must be maintained, because artists come and go,[51] some die,[52] and, at the same time, the group is crossed, even inhabited and invested, by others: notably the *Becs-Salés*,[53] the *Incohérents*,[54] and the *Zutistes*;[55] a dissident paper is even started: *La Vie drôle, gazette chatnoiresque* [*The Funny Life, Blackcattish Gazette*], which publishes eleven issues.[56]

However, once past its "heroic period,"[57] a necessity for decentralization, for turning toward the periphery, makes itself felt. The new series of *Le Chat Noir* thus turns to its colleagues in the Midi, the Félibrige, notably by means of the weekly "Chronique félibréenne—Lettres du Félibre."[58] This link between *Le Chat Noir* and the Félibrige is nothing new: in 1884, an entire issue of *Le Chat Noir* was devoted to it.[59] Moreover, the paper had been redesigned for the occasion, changing for the only time in its history its frontispiece into a dedication to Mistral, with the caption "Être Félibre ou mourir!" [Be Félibre or die!]. After this special issue, the collaborations are numerous. That said, this "Chronique félibréenne," consisting of an epistolary exchange between the staff of *Le Chat Noir* and Auguste Cavalier, which announces the research and progress of the Félibrige,[60] clearly denotes an appeal for help from external groups, to bring new life to the then aging paper: "Can you bring, at the same time as your southern song, a ray of warmth from that Provence sun of which we here have only a copied caricature."[61] The overture is confirmed by the addition of another rubric, unthinkable at the beginnings of the paper, "*Le Chat Noir* en Province,"[62] in which are published the latest news, publications, etc., of papers that could be called "cousins."

By these variable movements of connection, whose contours are undecidable, often schematic, even artificial, it is above all a question of the group inscribing itself in a careless and free apprehension of the world, outside the limited stability of official poets, outside the established genres.

To create its own dynamism so as to avoid being swept away in its turn by a logic that is already established, the linear and expedient one that consists of placing oneself "in the shadow of a great man."[63]

By way of conclusion, we would like to examine more closely the end of *Le Chat Noir*. The paper seems in fact to give one final swipe of the paw at the tacit approval of an exclusive group and its "creation unique in the world."[64] *Le Chat Noir*, already weakened, perishes for good, but in a way worthy of it, in the most thorough contradictions. So that Willy denounced in an article the pervasive artistic *panurgisme*,[65] and an insert concerning manuscripts sent to the paper is published in these terms: "We do not demand, from our future collaborators, dull and servile imitations of the remarkable works that have already appeared in the paper. It is not absolutely necessary that the manuscripts submitted be complete reproductions of joyful articles by Allais, Auriol, etc., etc."[66] One of the last issues of the *Nouveau Chat Noir*[67] launches a new rubric, supposedly "at the request of a large number of our subscribers": "The retrospective *Chat Noir*," in which will be published "poems and stories chosen from the former collection of *Le Chat Noir*," especially "Confession d'un Bec-salé"[68] [Confession of a Boozer]. Although absolutely lazy, this editorial decision would have had the merit of granting the paper one final connection with its distant and vibrant past. We have come full circle, one last time.

CHAPTER TWO
The Reader Has Le Chat Noir's Tongue

Rodolphe Salis, Harlequin is not kind to Pierrot (inventory number 704), Musées de Châtellerault, © Nicolas Mahu.

The paper *Le Chat Noir*, like all "little" magazines, is a forum where artists of the same group write and respond to one another, directly, as in dedicating poems for example, or indirectly, as in stories in which some colleague is cast in imaginary adventures.[1] If the dialogism between artists assumes a dominant place in the paper, encouraged by the demands of group cohesion, the "average" reader also seems to be solicited, provoked, and called to participate. The paper also plays with the formulaic rubrics of the press, having as much fun with its readership as with itself: reader mail, correspondence, classified ads, contests. These are, at their own level, representative of the space conceded to the reader's voice in exchange for a rabbit.[2] For it is crucial, in a broader sense, to fill the empty spaces on the page.

In keeping with the *fumiste* spirit that inhabits the paper, this interaction between writer and reader is "reflected once, twice, even ten times,"[3] that is to say indirect, rather than differentiated. It consists of a game of rebounds, and, in this way, catches the latter in a trap. Our hypothesis is that the reader becomes a sounding board for the specific vacuity of the imbecilic *chatnoiresque* humor—which is characterized by a trompe-l'oeil posture, due to its "naive"[4] appearance and its "fundamental skepticism";[5] it can then only provoke an "undecidable"[6] laugh. Mystification—the rabbit "proposed" to the reader (with a pun on *poser un lapin*, to stand someone up)—only takes effect later, in an "unexpected"[7] way. Whether it occurs by means of his laughter or by his speaking missing words aloud, in an involuntary and instinctual response, the mystification disseminates outside the journal the collective pleasure of exploring the void.

The reader: a "chatnoiresque Oedipus"[8]

Despite the title it displays, *Le Chat Noir* is dotted with many empty spaces, which take different forms. The reader is invited to decipher them or not, which is why the writers enjoy comparing him to Oedipus.

Such are Chapter III of Alphonse Allais's "Un drame bien parisien"[9] [A Thoroughly Parisian Drama], composed entirely of two lines of dots; the twisting sentences of Léon Gandillot's "L'homme le plus spirituel de Paris"[10] [The Wittiest Man in Paris], in which only the first letter of each word can be read; or the last two verses of Mélandri's "Sonnet-fantôme"[11] [Ghost-Sonnet]:

« !...(?) — !! — ...!. »
« —...¡¡¡..¿...!... — »

These voids also appear in wordless picture stories, particularly in those of Willette, whose *Pierroglyphique*[12] [Petroglyphic] writing still remains to be deciphered. Although this "ablation of texts"[13] allows the emergence of "a world in which that instrument of reason, the word, fades away, to dissolve into feelings and images,"[14] the readers, disconcerted, demand a translation. Émile Goudeau, then the chief editor of the paper, ends by giving the following explanation:

"A few myopic or simply meticulous minds, [...] would like to read the explanatory captions under his drawings. / That is impossible, dear readers, both you who only read us occasionally, and you fanatical subscribers [...], that is impossible because our artistic collaborator Willette [...] refuses. / And he refuses, O terrible subscribers, because it would spoil the appearance of his page of drawings. Question of art!"[15]

At a time when censorship, demanding self-censorship, rages,[16] these empty spaces prove in addition a good way to subvert it. By pretending to spare readers, and more precisely female readers, a few licentious or crudely corporeal scenes, it is frankly up to their writers to depict the omission. Take the "Gloria in Excelsis"[17] by Gaston Dumestre, which is meant to evoke the deflowering of a young woman: after the first phrase ("Gloria at last to your sex, etc."), it is nothing but a series of ellipses ironically mimicking the shape of the Catholic cross:

VI

GLORIA IN EXCELSIS (suite)

Gloire enfin à ton sexe, etc. . . . .
. . . .
. . . .
. . . .
. . . .
. . . .
. . . .
. . . .
. . . .
. . . .
. . . .
. . . .
. . . .

The motif of virginity thus takes on its full meaning in the textual void that depicts it: the poem recalls that the hymen is itself a deceptive surface, which bursts at the slightest contact and opens onto the void, like a simple joke. In "Histoire triste"[18] [Sad Story] by René Stalin, the dots themselves participate in a suggestion, both visual and sonic, of the lowly productive act: "Je réfléchis / Je fléchis / Je ch…" [I reflect / I bend / I sh…]. Although the writer stresses in a note that "the boldness of the rhyme compels him to leave it to be guessed by the sagacity of his female readers," the pseudo-polyptoton accompanied by an ellipsis after "ch…" depicts the fragmentation of the idea weakening into formlessness, like the decay of the rich rhyme toward its anagrammatic reversal.

Consequently, the reader is unceasingly called to guess what is hidden behind those blanks, and to read between the lines: everything is done to "excite his curiosity, his ingenuity."[19] The puzzle contests, a standard feature of the popular press, work in this way: they are composed of empty spaces to be filled by the reader. Organized by Jules Jouy in 1884, under the title of "Weekly Puzzle," they take different forms. There is at first a "puzzle" that consists of the construction of "a phrase in which a famous man's name will be pronounced, without it being exactly or inexactly written."[20] For the first name given—NABUCHODONOSOR [Nebuchadnezzar]—the solution chosen is the following: "Cosaque, ton cheval N'A BU QU'AU DON, AUX EAUX rapides; il ignore le goût de celles du Rhône."[21] [Cossack, your horse only drank at the Don, of the rapid waters; he does not know the taste those of the Rhone.] A month later, the puzzle evolves and becomes "The Game of Edgar Poe."[22] To win, one must "reconstitute a famous phrase, in which several letters have been removed and replaced by an equal number of dots," for example: ".A…E .E .EU.. M…M. ..T .O..E,"[24] which gives, in the next issue: "Madame se meurt! Madame est morte!" [Madame is dying! Madame is dead!]. This game is finally replaced by that of the Abbé Delille; one must "guess the meaning of poetic hieroglyphics,"[25] that is, solve a riddle posed in the form of a distich. For example: "Debout près du foyer qu'un autre Éole embrase, / Sombre, un autre Vulcain arme un autre Pégase"[26] [Standing by the hearth that another Aeolus sets ablaze, / Somber, another Vulcan arms another Pegasus] has as its solution "Blacksmith."[27] If these games are created with the intent to "Exercise, every week, the remarkable sagacity of the readers of Le Chat Noir,"[28] those launched almost ten years later aim to "bring to light many talents as genuine as they are unknown, and to stimulate the ardor of young writers."[29] The reader is called to create, and even collaborate on the paper, since the winning work is published. The drawing contest of 1893[30] is thus won by Louis-Gautier with a "Modern Leda,"[31] showing a naked young woman pressing a black cat to herself. In 1895, the paper launches several contests, among them a "humorous sonnet"[32] to be realized from given rhymes; thus is published "Caelum et terram"[33] by E. T. The reader's voice finds itself then a priori guided and instilled into the paper in homeopathic doses, within clearly defined spaces. It thus appears in the allotted context of answers to puzzle contests, as well as in that conceded to the integration of the winning work, whether poem or drawing, without however setting specific patterns: the spirit of the paper is instilled at this level, and sustained, in an avowed interdisciplinarity.

Elsewhere, riddles pop up at the whim of the texts, taking the reader by surprise. They are more rhetorical than anything else, and serve to boost the cohesion between the editorial staff and the readership. They can become ritualized running gags, based on knowing winks between initiates that develop into jokes known to all, like the pleasantries at the expense of Francisque Sarcey: "The editors of Le Chat Noir offer a prize of five hundred francs to the person who can guess the reason for our dedications to the late Francisque Sarcey during the year 1887."[34] Sometimes, certain writers assume the topos of a failed writer, mimicking one who loses his copy, and forgets what he wanted to write. They then call on the reader to correct, complete, and even choose in their place texts for which they sometimes deny all responsibility. For example, Willy, in a comic story,[35] pretends to confuse escarmouche [skirmish] with escarboucle [carbuncle], and asks the reader to find the better term to describe the eyes of "some mature and brunette matron." Sipert, for his part, after having evoked the death of one of his acquaintances, finds that "Spring Evenings" is finally unsuitable as a title: "I see that I have put at the top of my copy a title that has nothing to do with the subject treated, but it is too late to correct it, and besides, you are free, if you like, to put another in its place."[36] Let us also cite a fable by Willy,[37] whose moral is to be discovered:

> FABLE.
> Porel.
> Harel.
> Géraudel.
> MORAL:
> ?
> Find a word that rhymes; I have none under my pen.

In this other example, the reader is tacitly "requested" to recompose a missing line in the poem "Désespérance"[38] [Despair], a parody of Moréas's style in his collection "Le Pélerin passionné" [The Passionate Pilgrim], (1891):

> Mon âme est comme un vieux soulier
> Éculé de rêves d'or et d'espérances vaines;
> Plus d'amour, plus de joies sereines;
> .... (1)
> Plus de parfums d'héliotrope ou de verveines,
> Mon âme est comme un vieux soulier.
>
> [My soul is like an old shoe
> Worn down with golden dreams and vain hopes;
> No more love, no more calm joys:
> .... (1)
> No more perfumes of heliotrope or verbena,
> My soul is like an old shoe.]

Even if, for once in the paper, the note—"The reader is requested to reconstitute himself this line, before which the typesetter, like the famous flood, recoils in fright"—does not particularly invite the reader to show much flair for the subject.

Playing on the lack of replies from the readership to these riddles that are none, the writers routinely order their readers to answer. So, in the "Political Bulletins of Le Chat Noir," signed by a certain G***, it is written that if they want to know his name, "it is up to the readers to reply."[39] And the writers also routinely mock the tics of performative writing, of monologues or comic stories: the writer, calling out to the reader in rhetorical flourishes of "I ask you," adds in a note: "It is certain that none will have the courtesy to answer me."[40] The reader's voice in fact intervenes in sinuous and unexpected ways.

A Reader Whose Tongue Must Never Be Tied

According to these writers, it is not enough to entertain the reader. For this reason, they incite him to make his voice heard more precisely, by means of words or phrases, and to accomplish this they put in place a certain number of strategies.

Charles Aubertin, in an article,[41] reiterates that texts can effectively create a bond between writers and readers, but that it is most often a solely sonorous bond: the latter "guffaw noisily" and "double over with great noise." The reader's voice then seems at first to consist of the emission of inarticulate sounds, which, as they ring out, reverberate with the disarticulation of the words. After having made the reader read between the lines, or rather between the dots, these artists then strive to shift the lines, to make them overflow, to project them outside the paper: the reader's voice goes beyond its sole function of emitting a laugh. It is as good a way as any to "turn the world upside down,"[42] a world in which reading provokes the emission of a word which, like the *fumiste* laugh, is ambivalent, foolish, and even more, irrepressible.

Certain texts complicate the reading. Mental gymnastics no longer suffice, and the reader is pushed to pronounce physically certain words, indeed, whole pages. An entire issue is thus devoted to reformed spelling,[43] which would return to writing what is heard in the oral, that is, phonetic writing. "On écrira com on parl, é person ne san trouvera plu mal,"[44] [One will write as one speaks, and no one will be the worse for it], Francisque Sarcey summarizes in the editorial. To use simplified spelling is an opportunity to mock, among others, François Coppée, and his taste for words with sophisticated spelling: "Copé, lui, pleur de ce kil ny a kun h a ftisi. Si on lécoute, on écriré phthisie, pourkoi pa phthishie pandan kil y é?" [Coppée, he, complains that there is only one h in phtisie. If we listened to him, we'd write phthisie, why not phthishie while he's at it?]. In this case, it is the convoluted complexity of artistic writing that necessitates, for certain words, the reflexive effect of an oral reformulation on the part of the reader, to facilitate his reading. The words thus pronounced can be heard by anyone present in his surroundings. This assumes a more comical character in "Grain d'émétique"[45] [Grain of Emetic] by S. Daudé:

Veule, une carpe sans vergogne,

Qui dans l'eau puante se meut,
S'efforce de grimper et veut
Aux asticots mêler sa trogne.

Au fil du courant, un (1)
—Superbe flottaison gluante—
Un modèle luisant et rond,
S'engouffre en sa gueule béante.

[…]

Le bourgeois, toujours méprisant,
Qui me lira, certes, aura l'air de
Se dégoûter en me lisant,
Mais il bouffera, les prisant,
L'asticot, la carpe et la (2).

[Listless, a shameless carp,
Which moves in the stinking water,
Tries to rise and wants
To mix its face among the worms.

Drifting downstream, a (1)
—Superb gummy flotation—
A glistening and round model,
Is swallowed by its gaping maw.

[…]

The bourgeois, always disdainful,
Who will read me, certainly, will appear to
Be disgusted while reading me.
But he will eat, prizing them,
The worm, the carp, and the (2).]

These "grains of emetic"—which are the footnotes[46] substituted for the missing words, prosody, and rhymes—permit the reader to "taste" the scatological terms, the better to regurgitate them. The reader is in effect tricked by the irrepressible urge to pronounce these two words aloud, as in an aside, but impulsively, on the bounds of onomatopoeia: one can only imagine him saying with an astonished but satisfied air, after less than a minute, "*étron!*" [turd!] and then "*merde!*" [shit!], and then looking like a rude character to those around him. Reflexively, the joke only takes effect somewhat later. The dirty words appear in a rebound, between the writer who lets them "fall" on the page and the reader who picks them up and pronounces them, before sending them into the ears of someone nearby, who only hears an oath. This last is also tricked: he is still implicated in poetry, poetry that is disarticulated, fragmented, purged, of which nothing remains but its imbecilic and vulgar trappings.

It is not for nothing that Paul Héon warns the reader "against one of the most serious drawbacks of carelessness,"[47] which is, "one day of absent-mindedness, to forget your tongue, on the seat of a bus, for example, or elsewhere." Impossible then to "lick a stamp," to "stick out your tongue at the Police Commissioner," or to offer "the friendly exercise" to young ladies; one might add: to read *Le Chat Noir*! The reader's tongue is in fact as essential as the writer's. Let us recall that reading aloud was made a principle of the *Chat Noir* cabaret. The writers themselves read their texts on a stage allotted for that purpose, on the lines of the *Hydropathes*, which marks the beginning of performance poetry, as well as the fin-de-siècle monologue, centered around Charles Cros and Coquelin Cadet: communication is made "in the immediacy of the word."[48] Because it is a question of speaking what is habitually read, logic requires that the reader also speak, even if, as we have seen, it amounts to "speaking to say nothing."[49]

To do this, the writers amuse themselves by inserting little tricks for the better pronunciation of their texts: "NOTICE FOR THE READER OR PERFORMER.—To read or perform well what follows, it is highly recommended to make the voice quiver in the throat, to say L'AMOUL for L'AMOUR, to pronounce X as Z, to vibrate the Rs."[50] The voice must reverberate in the throat, assume a physical aspect; it is a question of gargling with the texts, since it is their resonance that matters, more than their (non) sense. These instructions from the writer also permit a double reading. For example, to the epigraph that heads one of his stories from "across the Channel": "Des ales! Des ales! (Michelett)"[51] [Ales! Ales! (Michelett)], Alphonse Allais recommends in a note: "Pronounced ailes [wings]." He therefore places as a motto, along with the joke on the pronunciation of the drink, a pun on a verse from a work by Jules Michelet, "L'Oiseau"[52] [The Bird]. Vocal delivery is also taken into account. Casting an ironic look at the long sentence—ten lines—that he has just written, Willy uses the opportunity to drum up a little publicity for himself:

"Anyone who can deliver this sentence in one go, without taking a breath, will receive as a prize one of the best works by our editor in chief, *Maîtresse d'Esthètes* [Mistress of Esthetes], the curious *roman à clef* published recently by Simonis Empis."[53]

Intensity, finally, is specified: the writers incite that quintessentially mute entity that is the reader to speak the texts by shouting them, which is not without recalling the verses of Raoul Ponchon: "If the dumb could speak / They would howl like the deaf."[54] This brings us back again to certain poets of the cabaret—Marie Krysinska and Maurice Rollinat, notably, shout their texts[55] —and places the reader in an identical position. A "Contest to earn the grade of carrier-crier for the paper *Le Chat Noir*"[56] is thus launched. If every crier is not *a priori* a reader but a vendor, one of the qualities required for a crier for *Le Chat Noir*—and this, exclusively—is precisely to be a reader of the paper. One one hand, the contest is addressed solely to readers and subscribers, on the other hand, having earned or working for "a doctorate of letters, doctorate of sciences, doctorate of law, or doctorate of medicine" is stated as necessary. In short, one must prove a certain education. The contest comprises two tests, the second of a metamedia order, since it consists of shouting "several times a minute: Just out! *Le Chat Noir*! The Delauby affair. M. Paul Héon arrested. Ten centimes!" The rules are stringent about potential cheating: "All syrups, tablets, gargles, or other pharmaceutical preparations capable of tricking the jury about the vocal powers of candidates are strictly forbidden." The use of the word "tricking" here is to be underlined: it echoes the hoaxes played not only in the paper, but in the words to be uttered. By reflex, the reader's voice is thus designated as facetious as those of the writers.

The Collective Pleasure of Exploring the Void

Paul Masson, in one of his "Affaiblismes" [Enfeebledisms], stresses that "in all hoaxes there is one imbecile, and more often two".[57] This idea can be found applied to the relationship between writer and reader. It is notably exemplified in the "Journal"[58] of Faux-Nohain. He denounces his "illustrious contemporary X...," whom he calls a "fool." A footnote on the person's identity—"put here any illustrious name you like; but not mine, eh? No kidding!"—thus enjoys showing a reader who could beat the writer at his own game. The joke, which "does not so much hide a presence as display an absence,"[59] can only reverberate in the reader's voice, which is also displayed, since it is exaggerated, even though it basically says nothing. The reader, made into a sounding board, becomes paradoxically the privileged speaker. We return to the definition of fumisme, as given by Georges Fragerolle: "To make someone feel, in a large group, by a series of words, that he is an imbecile, is the nature of wit. To agree with him and hand him the very quintessence of his imbecility, is the nature of fumisme."[60]

All distinctions between jokers, for example writer and reader, and consequently their voices, become blurred. The interest is no longer in knowing who laughs at what, or whom, but simply to laugh, and especially to spread this laughter to everyone, whether in one direction or another. The allusions to the reader's voice thus function to make the joke take hold, so it can grow, in other words to grant it more importance. So, in "Notre plébiscite,"[61] by P. H. (Paul Héon):

"In the course of the seventy-eighth installment of *Rome*, by M. Émile Zola (see *Le Journal* of March 11), the principal character in the book, the Abbé Pierre, asks himself, without answering it, the following question: 'Can I accept being a shuttlecock volleyed by all battledores?' / It seemed to us that this was a most delicate matter of conscience, whose solution would be particularly interesting. / That is why, reiterating and generalizing this question, we ask in turn: / 'Can one accept being a shuttlecock volleyed by all battledores?' / We request our readers to let us know their thoughts on the matter."

This text is a mise en abyme of the imbecilic chatnoiresque humor: it is a question of echoing a reflection (Zola's) devoid of interest to these artists, then reformulating it as a rhetorical question, and finally to pretend to await an answer that—according to the old formula, "stupid question, stupid answer"—would be just as hollow. The battledore and shuttlecock metaphorize these rebounds: the verb "volley" establishes the connection "reflected once, twice, often ten times"[62] of fumisme. This text is a joke in a joke in a joke; it would be hard to say whether Zola, the reader, or Paul Héon himself is the most duped: all is played out in this reflexive movement, which represents a joke exhausted to the maximum, from issue to issue.

The voice of the *Chat Noir* reader bears witness to the collective pleasure of exploring what plays out in the openings in the text, the better to resonate the void. Puzzle contests, empty spaces left for the reader, the voice amplified hyperbolically but never effectively, all participate in the representation of a generalized joke, consisting of texts inflated with air, that end in an explosion of laughter. The reader's voice, whether in inarticulate, fragmented, or howling form, can just as well drive away eventual future readers or subscribers as assemble them like a domestic crier, that is, domesticated without being muzzled. Let us remember that the paper *Le Chat Noir* claims to be the "Organ of Montmartre Interests."[63] By giving the reader a voice, by having him replay certain texts, or bits of text, at home, it consequently mimics, even as it prolongs it, its will to serve its own purpose and to attain universality.

CHAPTER THREE
Fumisme Is Not Just Men's Business!

"We were more than four or five."

"Smoke strong Turkish cigarettes and then waltz."

"The ultimate for a fumiste woman?
She dissipates whenever it's time to take a group photo!"

Fumiste women (illustration by the author)

The paper *Le Chat Noir*, in keeping with the spirit of the cabaret, itself inherited from the traditional men's club, establishes a context of exaggerated misogyny, "a noisy and joyful society of young men."[1] The texts grind out the usual clichés of the fin-de-siècle female figure: woman lies, her body is endlessly deconstructed, the lyric statement becomes a male consensus against Her—"The *Odor / Di femina*, vital dawn or soft death…"[2] writes Jérôme Nau. These accusations inevitably affect any woman who presents herself as a poet. The goal in effect is to seduce an audience and readership that is essentially male, in the image of the poets themselves. So while some writers evoke the "contemporary bluestockingism"[3] that seems to contaminate all literature with the turn of a play on words, others prefer a frontal and personal attack, like Franc-Nohain, who often targeted Marie Krysinska.[4]

Nevertheless, contempt for the woman poet is not the majority opinion in the paper. Women even seem rather well received. As it says in an article on the ninth exposition of the union of women painters and sculptors, "we are not among those precious nincompoops who guffaw at the idea of a woman doing an artist's work."[5] According to the logic of a group that claims to be different, and that extols eccentricity from all official, serious, and normal discourse, the woman poet, then considered the quintessential "other," can only find a place. Therefore women do publish their works, essentially poems. It is obviously not a question of a *chatnoiresque* female micro-society: certainly, these poets' texts are printed next to men's writings, but, with a few exceptions, remain rare, even insignificant. They nevertheless attract attention. Besides, in such a context, the presence of women emphasizes the questions of singularity and alterity at the core of *chatnoiresque* lyricism. Given this, how could one be "the other" in a group that never ceases to insist on its difference?

This study proposes to isolate female poetic production in the paper that concerns us, then to explore these women poets' assimilation of the new esthetic called fumisme, before analyzing the ambiguous and singular use they make of it. Our hypothesis is that the fumiste poem constitutes the masked space of the woman poet's first step to emancipation.

Context

Marie Krysinska, called "the Calliope of the *Chat Noir*,"[6] for she was an emblematic figure at the cabaret, and the only woman poet to contribute regularly to its related paper, emphasizes in a critical study how it was a "curious thing: up to the end of the *Chat Noir*, the female element was represented exclusively by the type of the comrade-woman, a rival on the field of artistic conquest: it was limited to four or five figures at most."[7] In fact, there were a few more than "four or five." It is fitting first to recall who these women are, and to review succinctly what led them to publish in this paper that was both artistic and marginal—at the beginning, at any rate.

From the first issues of the paper, we can count three women, then more or less known in the literary field at the time. They belong to bohemia, and frequent this milieu even before *Le Chat Noir* is launched and they become regulars in its eponymous cabaret. This is the case with Nina de Villard, who holds her own salon with her husband, Hector de Callias, from 1863 to 1882, attended by, among others, the future participants of the first *Chat Noir*: Charles Cros, Maurice Rollinat, and Émile Goudeau. Amélie Villetard is the first wife of Jules de Marthold, who also publishes poems in *Le Chat Noir*. As for Marie Krysinska, poet and musician, she participated in the meetings of the *Hydropathes*, the group that preceded the *Chat Noir*, where she wrote music for her peers' poems as well as her own, and took part in the exuberant and riotous dynamism of the group, crying, even "howling" her texts, and banging on the piano keys;[8] furthermore, she led the battle for free verse, beginning in the 1890s. When *Le Chat Noir* starts to become professional, several more established women writers, who publish in more institutional papers, also contribute: Jeanne-Thilda, alias Mathilde Stevens, both a novelist for *Gil-Blas* and an art critic, and Rachilde, a renowned novelist actively involved in the more serious *Mercure de France*. The paper's columns eventually welcome poems by personalities from the performing arts as well, such as Irma Perrot, actor and creator of the illustrated song, and Marie-Louise Bergeron, a lyricist whose texts appeared in *L'Ouest-artiste: gazette artistique de Nantes*. From this enumeration, we can at once make several observations. We note the diversity of personalities that are present, and the absence of a hierarchy based on symbolic capital: unknowns mix with those who have already made a name, in keeping with what also occurs among their male colleagues in *Le Chat Noir*. But, unlike these, the woman poet does not assume an imaginative or enigmatic pseudonym, which changes with the rubric or the theme to be treated—like A'Kempis, Miahou, or Sam Weller: she clearly signs her first and last name, and if there is a pseudonym, it is used consistently. This indicates a real determination to inscribe oneself as a poet, to make a name in the proper sense of the term, to distinguish oneself, and this without the boasting or play-acting that men can allow themselves.

In fact, however, ludic techniques and histrionics are not barred from female poetic production. Quite the contrary: they occur on the field of writing and beyond. In effect, if these women want to position themselves as much as "comrade(s)" at the heart of the group as "rival(s) on the field of artistic conquest"[9] more broadly in the literature of their time, the social dimension intervenes at the very core of their creation. If it is a question of going against the grain of lyrical convention, in particular, by shaking its foundations with parody, and by dismantling and profaning the traditional forms and conventional outlines that had become automatic reflexes of writing, it was also necessary, to participate fully in the group's activities, to adapt to a social *habitus*, to a presentation of oneself and one's art, to a comportment and system of values. In short: to adopt the *fumiste* posture, rather than a simple esthetic.

A Paradoxical Conformity to a Male Practice: *Fumisme*

This notion of posture is besides pointed out by Georges Fragerolle, when he attempts a definition of *fumisme*: "To be a good *fumiste*, it is often indispensable to be a lion covered in an ass's skin."[10] Reading this, we could translate it in these terms: *fumisme* functions as a deceptive device, in the service of an idiotic laugh. This laugh would be evoked by utilizing, as Bernard Sarrazin analyzes it, a "mixture of the serious and the light, the comic and the tragic, permitting a thousand effects, from subdued melancholy to sarcastic or burlesque discordance,"[11] or, in other words, by avoiding the habitual. However, *fumisme* is not based solely on mockery of all serious discourse; it works by means of mystifications, incongruous poems, nonsensical stories, and paradoxes, to evoke a laugh of rupture, that is rebellious, dark, sometimes involuntary, leading to "the somewhat sophisticated pleasure of escaping the constraints of sense, the pleasure of the undecidable."[12]

At the *Chat Noir*, alterity is affirmed first of all as antagonism for all poetry identified as official or major. It is for this reason that the group allows, in spite of everything, women to free themselves from the norm. Since it is true that, to place themselves outside poetic conventions, and outside the writing called feminine, which then had the reputation of being neither comic, erotic, nor bacchanalian—men limited it in effect to songs of nature, home, and family love—these women's challenge is made paradoxically by conforming to a type of writing essentially forged by men, but with new and subversive codes.

Because of this, they enter into the spirit of the audacities required at the *Chat Noir,* in particular joining in their hoaxes—Marie Krysinska thus publishes a false "study-preface," with supporting examples, of the work of a nonexistent poet, Anatole Galureau[13]—which can be found even in their poetry, giving it the form of a foolish joke, or an absurd and unpredictable story. So, one of Amélie Villetard's poems, appropriately entitled "Sincerités.—Rêverie,"[14] is, by its brevity—it is a dizain—particularly rooted in the genre of the joke. The misdirection rests on the fact that the intimate *rêverie* leads to the memory of a sight whose horror is used to subversive effect:

J'aime à me promener, à la fin d'un beau jour,
Dans le quartier lointain qui s'étend tout autour
Du champ de Mars, dans ce vieux faubourg de Grenelle
Où se dresse parfois la porte solennelle
D'un hôtel blasonné. [...]
C'est là que, l'autre soir, entre deux balivernes,
Un beau jeune homme imberbe, aux jambes en cerceaux
Découpait un enfant en tous petits morceaux.

[I like to walk, at the end of a beautiful day,
In the distant neighborhood that extends all around
The Champ de Mars, in this old suburb of Grenelle
Where sometimes there arises the solemn door
Of an emblazoned hotel. [...]
It was there that, the other evening, between two trivialities,
A handsome young beardless man, with bandy legs,
Was cutting a child into tiny pieces.]

The macabre clashes with the lightness of the language, in the parodistic gap between the stylistic form of precious lyricism and the morbid content. *Fumisme* thus upsets the system of values, and troubles the surface of speech as well as the poetic genre. A shift from a poetry that is solemn, chiseled, and grandiloquent, toward futility, lightness, and, above all, duplicity, is thus orchestrated, which also entails a resort to popular and minor forms like the song or the ballad,[15] or brief forms like the dizain, and to shorter meters like the octosyllabic. Profaning art becomes a prerequisite, and creation then merges with a taste for negation, as Nina de Villard emphasizes when she rhymes *artiste* with *nihiliste* in "Une Russe"[16] [A Russian Woman].

It is precisely the incongruity of the lyric subject that transgresses a whole tradition, both masculine and feminine, in which the women poets see themselves trapped. So, although Marie-Louise Bergeron, in her poem "Pour chanter l'amour"[17] [To Sing of Love], seems to conform to the anti-love song characteristic of the paper—"I never sing of Love / Because I love no one"—the poem becomes rather the place for a metapoetical reflection on the carrying power of her own voice, judged by the leitmotiv that recurs at the end of each stanza: "One's voice is not beautiful enough / When one has never loved," for it is not "pure/sweet/strong/somber enough," respectively, according to the stanza. Indeed, for these women, it is a question of not confining the poetic text, or the elements ordinarily attributed to it, to the constraints of the roles prefabricated and imposed on women.

In more surprising ways, the women poets also assume male practices of writing and means of expression. They adopt men's attitude, borrowing a misogynistic, boorish, and bawdy tone. That translates, most notably, into putting the first person into the masculine. So, in Marie Krysinska's "Chant moderne,"[18] the "I" separates from his "cute one," and culminates in a final bit of boorishness in which he rids himself of the woman he no longer wants by offering her to someone else:

Qu'un autre prenne
Tes jolis yeux, petite mienne,
Et ta bouche amoureuse, si rouge aux blanches dents,
Je n'y vois pas d'inconvénient.

Et même au Cercle, je connais
Un qui te trouve un charme rare,
Je te présenterai
Comme par hasard.

[That another take
Your pretty eyes, my little one,
And your amorous mouth, so red with white teeth,
I have no objection.

And even at the Circle, I know
Someone who finds rare charm in you,
I'll introduce you
As if by chance.]

Marie Krysinska also uses this method in the medieval, or rather Renaissance, counterpart to this poem: "Chanson d'autrefois"[19] [Song of the Past]. This text, presenting an "I" who is considering suicide, but celebrating the love he knew with the "beautiful chatelaine," is also a way to denounce the failings of her current epoch, then advocating more discourteous love songs.

This does not mean, however, that these women praise a certain feminine ideal. On the contrary, they enjoy deflecting this ideal toward the grotesque, in keeping with the practices of degradation at the *Chat Noir*. Thus, women can be presented as stupid[20] (Krysinska), cruel and unfaithful, accumulating conquests[21] (Villard) and fleeting relations in the sole aim of obtaining "a moment of exhilaration"[22] (Jeanne-Thilda), in a "dark box seat"[23] even during the performance of a play! In "Sincérités—Simple histoire,"[24] Amélie Villetard reworks the taste for the carnivalesque favored by her colleagues at the *Chat Noir*. She shows woman oriented completely toward her lower body, as suggested by the subversion of the topos of female greed into gluttony:

Qui donc avait, du front de la jeune martyre,
Chassé si promptement la fatigue et le deuil,
Que chaque bâillement devenait un sourire?
C'était un pâtissier qui lui faisait de l'oeil.

[Who then had, from the young martyr's brow,
So quickly banished fatigue and grief,
That her every yawn became a smile?
It was a pastry cook making eyes at her.]

This is also emphasized by the unusual collusion of the motifs of marriage and prostitution, which consists of "Beneath the light of a lamppost, / Anyone can take her hand,"[25] in "Cœur mort" [Dead Heart] by Irma Perrot.

However, there are perceptible differences in their writings from those of their male counterparts: for these women, rudeness and misogyny do not reach the level of insult, nor even obscenity, that is a specialty of the periodical. Women laugh at Woman, in the same way that bohemians laugh at themselves.

Conformity to male practices corresponds to the essence of *fumisme*: for these artists, it is a question of appearing masked. *Fumisme* is thus reviewed and corrected from a female perspective and from another reading: paradoxically, it becomes changed itself.

An Ambiguous and Singular Use of
Fumisme

These poems are in fact more marked by references to female poetry than they seem. The borrowing of so-called "feminine" elements does not show femininity as much as a choice to reappropriate fixed motifs and renew them. We have decided to consider three of them: fabric, flowers, and the "I."

Let us begin with fabric. In "Les Bijoux faux"[26] [False Jewels], by Marie Krysinska, this motif serves to depict nature as a cheap imitation, with an ambivalence accented by the use of free verse:

Dans la clarté des lampes allumées,
S'épanouissaient des roses en satin et des camélias de velours.
Les feuilles étaient en fin papier luisant,
Et les tiges de laiton, soigneusement enveloppés de ouates et de taffetas.

[In the brightness of the lit lamps,
Bloomed satin roses and velvet camellias.
The leaves were of thin shiny paper,
And their stems of brass, carefully wrapped in cotton and taffeta.]

Krysinska uses the techniques and themes of both feminine and masculine lyricism, as well as the free verse that accentuates the ambiguity of the language, to parody and undermine feminine poetry, as imagined by men. It corresponds neither to the use men make of fabric—such as fetishism for the components of female lingerie—nor of that supposedly of women, but serves to embody the imaginary, and particularly to embody the mystification so prized by fumisme. If, for Charles Maurras, "it is a pleasure for women to match words like fabrics,"[27] women poets reply that the male subject is just as fascinated by this element. Amélie Villetard, in her poem "Désespoir"[28] [Despair], exaggerates this idea by invoking fabric—here, a blouse—as the necessary cause of disgrace, and from that to the final laugh. The man first appears in "crisis," as hysterical:

> Il parlait vaguement comme aux instants de crise,
> Disant: Je suis perdu! Je suis déshonoré!
> Ce matin, j'en suis sûr, c'est un fait avéré,
> Elle avait oublié de changer de chemise!

> [He spoke vaguely as in moments of crisis,
> Saying: I am lost! I am dishonored!
> This morning, I'm sure, it's a known fact,
> She had forgotten to change her blouse!]

Another motif of feminine poetry, flowers, is reworked and degraded in the *fumiste* manner, notably by Irma Perrot, in a poem with a revealing title—a question mark.[29] Flowers are profaned, "stripped of their petals" by a "nasty cricket," destroyed, poisoned, as if the woman poet took a malicious pleasure in deconstructing this topos, especially since she is spinning a metaphor of femininity:

> Deux amoureuses pâquerettes
> [...]
> Pour que l'on ne vît pas souillées

> Leurs voluptueuses pâleurs,
> Ont bu comme un poison les pleurs
> Dont leurs robes étaient mouillées.

> [Two amorous daisies
> [...]
> So that one might not see soiled

> Their voluptuous pallors,
> Drank like a poison the tears
> That wetted their dresses.]

The ambiguous and singular use that these women make of male practices goes beyond them, because they specifically borrow the clichés of so-called "feminine" lyricism, notably sincerity, introspection, or love. The *fumiste* attitude makes it possible for them to escape the limitations of the genre, as much sexual as poetic, and to create a poetic language that cannot be categorized, because it rests on the undecidable. For sincerity is substituted a duplicity that endlessly mirrors and multiplies itself, by polyphonic techniques, doubling the voices of these women in the manner of a laugh that never stops erupting, because of the play of echoes. It is therefore a question, in Marie Krysinska's "Ballade,"[30] of "the song of birds, and the foliage that whispers mysteriously and perfidiously," or of "mocking stars." The woman poet therefore lets out her laugh, irrepressible and incurable, which spreads throughout her whole being, shaking every part of her body, before reaching her voice: "Le Rire divin sonne de somptueux tocsins, / Les lèvres riaient, aussi les yeux, aussi les seins."[31] [The divine Laugh rings sumptuous tocsins, / The lips laugh, also the eyes, also the breasts.]

The "I" is obviously also implicated. In effect, and this was the focus of the criticism of the time, female writing was defined as a statement of the self and of the emotions, all exaggerated, narcissistic and falsified. So, according to Charles Maurras: "To say 'me' is almost part of woman's character. 'Me' bursts forth at every occasion in her speech, not as an auxiliary, not for convenience of language, but with that procession of blatant personal impressions that signify quite precisely: *me who is speaking, me and none other*."[32] The women poets of the *Chat Noir* therefore take this poetic of "me" in the opposite direction, which simultaneously allows them to rid themselves of the poetic habits of their male counterparts, who regularly use the lyrical subject, and to dismantle it more effectively.

Marie Krysinska, in particular, whose collaborators readily acknowledge that she is "concerned with the *never done*,"[33] makes of this "me" an infrequent and weakened part of her poetry, preferring indetermination. Her poetry is often unlabeled; in fact, she usually uses the impersonal or the third person plural, as in "Symphonie en gris"[34] [Symphony in gray]:

Les silhouettes vagues ont le geste de la folie.
Les maisons sont assises disgracieusement comme de vieilles femmes.
Les silhouettes vagues ont le geste de la folie. —
C'est l'heure cruelle et stupéfiante, où la chauve-souris déploie ses ailes grises, est s'en va rôdant comme un malfaiteur.
Les silhouettes vagues ont le geste de la folie.

[The vague silhouettes have the gesture of madness.

The houses sit awkwardly, like old women.

The vague silhouettes have the gesture of madness.

It is the cruel and stupefying hour, when the bat unfurls its gray wing, and goes off prowling like a criminal.

The vague silhouettes have the gesture of madness.]

On one hand, femininity is apparently not clearly claimed; on the other hand, this neutrality is based on common poetic forms, on rhythmic prose or free verse. Besides, it is her willingness to engage in this battle as a woman that harms Marie Krysinska. One of her defenders and colleagues at *Le Chat Noir*, Narcisse Lebeau, stresses this point in an article on the poetry collection *Rythmes pittoresques*, which had just been released:

"Also, as even the Symbolists admit, if Mme Marie Krysinska has been so casually excluded from articles that bang their bass drum about the new artistic preoccupations and new names, it is—solely—because she is a woman (no one is perfect!), but also perhaps because she had the indiscretion to be the first poet to liberate verse;—in other words: that she *imitated* the *Decadents* four years before the *Decadents* were born in literature."[35]

Mostly idolized at *Le Chat Noir*, while attracting critical wrath from other periodicals, she keeps at her personal writing, and even accelerates the pace of her contributions to the paper between 1889 and 1893, in the midst of the battle for free verse, to ensure herself a prominent role in this poetic innovation. The particularity of such writing is thus to be found in its level of audacity: in different degrees, it is shocking to assume one's own voice when mounting the stage of a cabaret, but also to claim a poetic innovation when one is a woman. One aspect of the poet's identity therefore seems realized by implication, parallel to the dismantling of expected clichés and norms, such as the use of the lyric subject, to affirm her own poetics.

The women poets of *Le Chat Noir*, following the example of their male colleagues, present themselves as unorthodox, and open up a wide range of possibilities in the matters of strategy, form, and polyphony. Besides, this duplicity, inherent in the posture that must be maintained to be heard in such a context, yields a double result: as practiced by these women poets, *fumisme* tends to affirm the singularity of their own voices—not only as women, but as poets. This undoubtedly works as a singular and specific strategy for emancipation: *fumisme* becomes a reflection on the ambivalent writing of feminine poetry, which, instead of trafficking in sensitivity, does not hesitate to pluck the sensitive string of the masculine lute.[36]

PART 2:

THE SUBVERSION OF THE SERIOUS DISCOURSE

CHAPTER FOUR
Money

LE CHAT NOIR

Passage de Venus sur le Soleil

A ma Julia chérie WILLETTE.

Seen as tyrannical and deceptive, the prime mover of decadence in both society and the arts, the symbol of the rising middle class, money is abundantly caricatured and mocked, as much in the texts as the illustrations appearing in the paper—as well as, in a more surprising way, at the core of the financial articles!

Here we shall explore these caricatural depictions of money, then analyze the subversion of the serious discourse accorded to money, by turning to the financial articles in *Le Chat Noir*, before shedding light on how this motif more deeply permeates the metapoetic texts, inasmuch as there is a shift in bohemia's relation to it, culminating in a change in what is called "poetic gold." For if laughter permits numerous games about money and the economic, societal, and political dysfunctions connected with it, it also seems to lead to the revelation of another crisis, more deeply affecting fin-de-siècle artists, that of the ideal.

The Fortune of the Motif of Money

The motif of money is presented by various emblems, whether physical, such as coins, or symbolic, by means of various archetypical figures. Presented as extravagant, even nightmarish, in the schematic *chatnoiresque* treatment, they invade the space of the texts and illustrations, expressing as much the omnipresence of money in society as its omnipotence.

Adept at literalism, the artists of Le Chat Noir obviously prefer to attack the coin, whether écu, franc, or gold louis. Laughter makes itself heard, dissonant and strident, incarnating as a stream of hard cash that contaminates the environment as well as living beings, which it transfigures. Minted in parodistic distortions, particularly enlargements, its size becomes enormous, and allows incongruous settings. Its round form inspires fantastic juxtaposition with the stars. A twenty-franc coin therefore occupies more than half of a drawing by Willette, "Venus Passing Across the Sun."[1] The inverse method of reduction is also used: a louis is defined as "a little pocket sun,"[2] whereas the moon takes the form of an écu, but a "cropped écu,"[3] altered. This new relationship with money corrupts human bodies as well as human relations. Man is first shown leading the world, waving his "hundred arms"[4] in Galice's drawing "Her Highness Woman"; the gold coins that stream from his body, like drops of sweat, are destined to satisfy only woman, because they fall in piles at her feet. Female venality is in fact often emphasized. In a drawing by Willette, her heart, beating only for gold, is even replaced by a large twenty-franc coin, the point of the drawing being the pun in the caption, which refers to Montmartre, the neighborhood of the Chat Noir: "Oh! Le Sacré-Cœur!"[5] Mythical female figures are also ridiculed in this way. This is for example the case with Salome. In a poem by Jean Lorrain,[6] the mythemes are updated into fin-de-siècle terms: John the Baptist is changed into Pierrot, which heightens his degradation in pantomime, whereas the sacred halo and standard crown are subverted into gold louis. The thirst for blood and vengeance, consubstantial with the figure of Salome, is replaced by a thirst for gold—with probable antisemitic implications:

La tête de Pierrot […] a pour nimbe un louis d'or;

Un louis… et, sous son fin maillot taché de boue
Et de sang, Salomé, fille et sœur de la Mort,
Rit à l'Humanité, que ce louis d'or bafoue.

[Pierrot's head […] has for a halo a gold louis;

A louis… and, under her thin singlet spotted with mud
And blood, Salome, daughter and sister of Death,
Laughs at Humanity, which this gold louis mocks.]

We find this fin-de-siècle Salome again, on the right in Willette's Te Deum laudamus, a stained glass window that adorned the ground floor of the cabaret, after its move in 1886 into the town house at 12 rue de Laval. The window taunts passersby, since enthroned in the center is a golden calf, seated on a safe and backed by a guillotine. The cabaret is undoubtedly answering, mockingly, its detractors who accuse it of becoming bourgeois, since the scene is a denunciation of the corrupting but unavoidable power of money. Besides Salome, the central figure is the golden calf, another symbol of the cult of money and material goods. It appears oblivious to the chaos that surrounds it—a woman strangles her child at its feet, workmen seem about to destroy it, etc. The scene is programmatic of the chatnoiresque treatment of this figure. In fact, although it is not destroyed, attacks are plentiful. The motif is interpreted in its literal sense, that is, as an animal. Henry D'Erville, in a poem on "The Crisis" in the farming community, plays on the youth of the animal, to proclaim the debility of the golden calf: "The golden calf is just a stillborn calf!"[7] But depictions also show it as older. Having become an ox, it is transposed to the context of the Carnival and the traditional processions of the "fatted ox."[8] Even more, its cult is turned into the adoration of beef, which is still reserved exclusively for the rich: "Him, he liked beef; however, he was rich when he died."[9] This opinion, pronounced ironically as a logical equation in a story by Albert Glatigny, by a father to his son, leads to a denunciation of the social separation between those who can eat beef and those who cannot, for it is well known that "they don't like beef, those artists!" The critique of the figure of the bourgeois finally culminates in the caricature—certainly topical—of him as bovine: "clumsy," walking "with heavy steps,"[10] he is even acclaimed by bovids, who recognize him as one of them: "Toi, que brame la vache aux pendantes mamelles; / Toi, que clame le boeuf amoureux de femelles."[11] [You, as the cow with pendulous udder bellows; / You, as the ox amorous of females proclaims.]

Because it can belong only to the rich, money is notable for its elusiveness, under the pens of bohemian artists. It is in turn won by chance in the lottery and then stolen,[12] replaced with a bottle of cognac in a story by George Auriol[13] or with stones by Maurice Mac-Nab.[14] Bad luck touches frugal characters as well. The calculation of their daily expenses takes an absurd turn. It becomes impossible in the eyes of Guilledou, because of the number of days in leap years.[15] Jean F.ʼ., on his part, sees his financial plans frustrated by a tax on bachelors that would cost him twenty francs. He therefore decides to marry, but marriage proves too expensive:

"Thirty francs! Twenty francs! Jean F.ʼ. examines himself, analyzes himself: his soul, like Buridan's soul long ago, is equally tempted by two solutions equally impossible to realize."[16]

He therefore buys a revolver and some cartridges with his savings, and commits suicide, prompting a new development in the story: "It was at around this time that the Chamber passed a tax on suicides." The motif of money alludes to a generalized mystification, which tricks the characters as well as the reader, because it forms a sort of spring needed to provoke the final laugh. The construction of the sonnet allows the effect to be measured. In "Funérailles,"[17] by Georges Boutteleau, the motif of money is not introduced until the final tercet, emphasizing that the cherubs, rather than preparing paradise to receive a new soul, are setting up a paying space:

> Devant ce paradis en frais,
> La pauvresse, perdant sa paix,
> Dit: Mon Dieu, comment vous paierai-je?

> [Before this fresh paradise,
> The poor woman, losing her composure,
> Says: My God, how will I pay you?]

In "L'âge d'or"[18] [The Golden Age], a wordless picture story by Willette, the cascade of vignettes that depict Pierrot trying to seduce a woman by various methods comes from the same effect: little does it matter if Pierrot throws himself at the woman's feet, sings her praises with a lyre or violin, paints her portrait, or threatens suicide. She remains indifferent to everything, except, in the last vignette, to the gold louis that Pierrot's skeleton extends to her from the grave he has dug himself. The punchline, brought on by the macabre exaggeration, reveals a double laugh, in terms of, precisely, the coin, simultaneously ludic and destructive.

Far from contenting themselves with simply mocking the central role that money assumes in society, the artists of *Le Chat Noir* attack the absurd potential of its practices, playing on different comic modalities. Furthermore, given that the discourse about money takes up more and more space in the media, because serious papers publish a rubric about it, the financial column, *Le Chat Noir*, which never tires of lampooning the codes of journalism, sets about producing one as well… which is worth its weight in gold!

Financial Columns

Throughout its existence, the paper publishes a weekly financial bulletin,[19] more or less serious, more or less codified, depending on the times. Rather than conforming, mockingly, to the media norms of the time, it is more a question of commenting on the economic crisis and scandals then shaking society, like the Panama scandal,[20] or a sluggish savings campaign exaggerated to grotesquerie in an article by Xernand Fau.[21] The financial columns of Le Chat Noir take the discourse to which they are conventionally devoted, and turn it against itself. The serious spirit is ridiculed, notably by the deliberate absence of precise or numbered data, as Moncrif explains in his bulletin "Finances": "We don't want to reason with numbers: it would be conclusive, but supremely tedious,"[22] making room for buffooneries:

"For the sole reason that we are in Carnival. This is a disguised way, readers, to tell you that I can find absolutely nothing serious to tell you. And, besides, the Exchange has not been the least bit serious this week. Did it not amuse itself by falling after an attack of influenza in the Emperor of Russia? Then it fell further at President Carnot's rheumatism."[23]

The Exchange itself is portrayed as a character from a farce, playing with the minor ailments of heads of state, and the calendar seems to attract the columnist's attention more than the stock prices. After Carnival comes Lent, with the result that "as a good Catholic, the Exchange fasted during the holy week."[24] The motif of the fool is revived under the likeness of Harlequin's costume, attributed to gold because of its rich colors, but also because of its phonetic associations, which form an offensive pun: "It come in all colors to suit all tastes: red gold, yellow gold, and... hard gold [or dure]."[25]

This joyful indifference to financial information contaminates the organization of the articles. Frequent metabasis, digressions, addresses to the reader, marks of orality, all have the effect of distorting the subject, thereon placed on a track whose only destination is laughter:

"And the English still turn up... new goldmines. It's getting pretty funny! All the same, eh? How many goldmines there are! And nobody suspected it. My God! Man is not a very serious creature! Nature puts a heap of gold at his disposition, in the form of mines, and he won't take it! It's enough to make you give up trying to help him."[26]

Common sense and logic are more specifically undermined in the articles written, parodistically, in the voice of an alley cat—a subversive motif if there ever was one, because of its connection to the anarchistic graphics, amplified by the play on the paper's name—Matou, who signs the "Miaulements financiers" [Financial Mewings]. The jargon of economics is reinvested and reduced to his level, resemanticized according to the feline vocabulary, either by the repetition of expressions already containing the word "cat," like "call a cat a cat and the financier X... a scoundrel,"[27] or by the reformulation of financial expressions consecrated by its addition: "one must be a cat clever in financial matters."[28] Rather than addressing the economic crisis, the appearance of cats acts as a barometer. So, as a consequence of a drop in prices and revenues, the cat at the discount bank "lets hang, like a weeping willow, its caudal appendage, which until recently affected the very elegant and refined shape of a hunting horn."[29] But it is above all cats' interest in "satisfaction, felt by their stomachs,"[30] otherwise known as food, to which the phenomena of the Exchange are reduced, and by which they are reinterpreted. Inflation in effect has consequences for Matou's diet: "It is well understood that a decline followed, which drove up the price of offal, and reduced my daily ration."[31] If Matou is at this point so well informed on business matters, it is because he happened to "lick a newspaper thrown in a garbage can."[32] That said, it is only after examining the meager leftovers that he can form an opinion on the seriousness of the crisis: "No more fishbones in the basket, that's a serious indicator, the bones are gnawed to the marrow. A bad business." Laughter confuses the trail, the words, the codes: in Le Chat Noir, laughing at money amounts to "speculating on words."[33] Besides, this procedure extends beyond the rubric devoted to it. A story by Henry Somm, for example, adapts the description of a character to the prevailing terms of the stock market: "The queen was as beautiful as a dividend."[34]

It is an irony of fate, however, that these financial bulletins, meant originally as a joke, become serious, documented, and analytical throughout the years. Although they establish a critique of money that is particular to Le Chat Noir, the stakes they reveal are no less true. In effect, the group never loses the view that this is not necessarily a laughing matter. The artist without a sou is not just a pose. Worse: the Ideal itself is bankrupt.

Poetic Gold, a Reviled Ideal

In Le Chat Noir, the motif of money is constantly compared to that of poetic gold, the only wealth that the bohemian artist possesses a priori. The subversions respond ironically to this double indigence into which respectable and bourgeois society has thrown him. In effect, poetic gold has only an outmoded value in the eyes of society, even if, paradoxically, verses are only "good for people who aren't hungry."[35] The image of the poet as a "superb beggar,"[36] "dining less often on beefsteak than on verses!"[37] persists. The fin-de-siècle poet appears torn between a thirst for the ideal and a desire for money, as a verse by Charles Cros emphasizes: "we dream of gold, of silver, of feasts."[38] A reevaluation of the value of poetic production takes the place of his search for the ideal, and the poet can only compare his collections to "an old pot full of louis,"[39] but worthless louis, despite his hard work. As Émile Goudeau recognizes, in the form of a story:

"He was a poet, and a poet overwhelmed by ideas, therefore overwhelmed by work. From morning to night he cultivated analysis, spaded synthesis, rigorously watered his well and duly worked rhymes. Now, this business of working hard both day and night, O labor of every minute! this hard business of a worker overwhelmed by work earned him nothing. […]

"Harassed by his boss the Ideal, jostled by his foreman Mr. Dream, always working the rugged paper with the plow of his muddy pen, always tying up packets of rhymes and stamping them with the seal of Imagination, then carrying them to the office […], he, A'Kempis, a poet who earned nothing from this curious job, looked enviously at people who had no work."[40]

The poets of *Le Chat Noir*, in fact, do not fail to announce the problems they encounter precisely in deriving profit from their works. Publicly demanding from an editor the money he owes becomes established as a new poetic motif. Verlaine, in a sonnet dedicated "to Léon Vanier, man of property,"[41] sarcastically proclaims the conditions under which he will accept to be published again by Vanier, exploiting the motif of the golden calf. He must be paid generously: "Let the calf be golden and quite fatted," for if Vanier does not obey—the game of variations around the (golden) calf and its alimentary meaning allows the poem to end with a joke—Verlaine refuses to let the reader—also swindled by the publisher—be able to say: "You'd think he was a *veau*! [which, as here, also means fool]."

As we can see, the motifs of the coin and the golden calf seep into the core of these metapoetic texts, to the point that the poetic material is resemanticized to that effect. Besides, the standard personnel of poetry is also rearranged. On one hand, the moon, the muse of noctambulant artists, the crucible of the Ideal and harmonious poetics, is strangely sublimated in a poem by Louis Denise:[42] it is "pale and round, appealing and wan, / Like an ideal écu of a hundred sous." But to praise it leaves a bitter, ambiguous, "metallic"[43] taste. On the other hand, the quest for poetic perfection is subverted by Jean Moréas into a "golden rhyme with a metallic timbre,"[44] suggesting a degradation, the "metallic" sound recalling the physicality of a coin. Finally the poetic terms themselves are parodied by recourse to the lexical field of finance. Fernand Chezell thus baptizes one of his poems "Rimes millionnaires,"[45] playing on the collusion between the stated—the topos of the venal woman—and the statement—the poem is comprised of rhymes called "millionaire" because they are very "rich"—that is, have at least four phonemes in common:

Il se peut que ta bouche rie,
Disant: C'est autant d'or de pris;
Mais je lâche ta boucherie,
Car tu vends ta chair hors de prix!

[Perhaps your mouth may laugh,
Saying: It is so much gold taken;
But I leave your butcher shop,
Because your flesh is too expensive!]

The strict usage of rhyme is turned into a game aiming to make it the pretext for the title, at the expense of the meaning, displaying an art of versification in crisis. Extending the rhyme in this way, limiting it to similar sonorities for an entire quatrain, portrays an esthetic impoverishment, symptomatic of the fin de siècle, echoing the attacks proclaimed against (high) lyricism—the *fumistes* declare war on this superstructure, in the hopes of letting all its sonorous hollowness ring out. Money not only besieges every stratum of society, it also overturns the language of poetry, up to its alchemical power of transformation, as Baudelaire had defined it: "I kneaded mud and made gold."[46] The transmutation from negative to positive becomes discredited by this monetary interference that the *Chat Noir* poets proclaim as generalized. A poem with an evocative subtitle, "Le Dieu jaune"[47] [The Yellow God], by Paul Marrot, evokes what is effected by the "blond idol" that "tient en ses flancs, enfouis, / Talismans, philtres inouïs." [holds in its sides, buried, / Talismans, extraordinary philtres.] According to him, money "transforme les "nons" en "ouis," / En palais les bouibouis." [transforms "nos" into "yeses," / Into palaces, cheap restaurants.] In other words, money discredits the Ideal that traditionally resides in Beauty, and, once the act of transformation is complete, restores only ugliness and mediocrity. In short, from money emerges the triumph of the grotesque… and the absurd! Because, as a corollary to the protest against money, another against poetic gold, aimed at even its production, is also demanded, by the poets themselves.

Although the modalities of the laughter targeting money are stated everywhere—exaggeration, caricature, mockery, irony, extending even to the structure of the text to trigger a punchline—and although the pronouncements and language of economics are themselves ridiculed by means of jubilant financial articles, and even reinvented in the terms of the paper's totem animal, the writers and artists of *Le Chat Noir* take a no less acerbic look at the patrimony that society has deigned to leave them: the quest for the Ideal, itself subverted and turned grotesque and derisive. Laughter at money thus turns back ironically on the fumiste artist himself, one of whose characteristics is laughing at himself, pushing subversion to its limits. In so doing, the mockery of economic and/or financial discourse becomes not just another way to ridicule all serious discourse. *Le Chat Noir* has in effect the audacity to reveal publicly and collectively the most prosaic and esthetic negotiations of self with self, as well as those with publishers, which are usually read only in novels and serials, not in poetry. Besides, it is not by accident that they unveil to the reader a materialistic approach to poetic production, to the point of making of it, in many fanciful texts, a lucrative merchandise manufactured in industrial ways. In one of them,[48] a sale is offered "wholesale to young magazines short on copy," and prices are posted—imaginary and quite modest, since they are for a hundred copies of the same sonnet—in black and white:

	On 4 rhymes	On 2 rhymes
Romantic sonnet	4 fr. 50	5 fr. 50
Parnassian sonnet	7 fr. 50	8 fr. 50
The same, polished model	8 fr. 50	10 fr. 50
Symbolist sonnet (verses guaranteed 14 feet minimum)	6 fr. 50	7 fr. 50
Symbolist sonnet with assonances	4 fr. 50	5 fr. 50

And obviously, as George Auriol ironically concludes in another text of this type: such an industry "is the height of art!"[49]

CHAPTER FIVE

Subverting Translation at the End of the 19th century: The Examples of Two *Chat-noiresque* Periodicals, *Le Chat Noir* (1882-1897) and *La Vie Drôle* (1893-1894).

Dieu et mon Droit ! --- Dessin de Ferdinandus.

For those who frequent *La Revue blanche* or *Le Mercure de France*, or papers of wider circulation like *La Revue des Deux Mondes*, the practice of translation into French in fin-de-siècle periodicals seems abundant, and even intensifies beginning in the 1890s. This marks an evolution in the status of both translations and foreign texts, not only in the literary field but within the media culture. This practice, dominated by contemporary works in English, German, and Russian, is part of a global movement toward cosmopolitanism. In the eyes of its producers, the importation of foreign literature would contribute to a renewal of the literary landscape. Even more, this initiative correlates with the editorial line of avant-garde papers, which also disseminate it, and whose vocation is publishing original work, since translation is then so considered. Obviously, such a plethora of material could not pass unnoticed, and it soon becomes the subject of parodies in the columns of the little papers themselves. At least, to our knowledge, in those of *Le Chat Noir*—one could extend this analysis to the satirical press of the period that interests us to gauge its specificity. Comic periodicals in effect do not think of themselves as places that allow this type of publication. In particular, a paper like *Le Chat Noir*, which crystallizes around its home base, Montmartre, proclaimed as an independent republic—whereas Paris is conceived as a distant foreign country, with customs as absurd as they are outmoded. From its first issue, the paper affirms itself as an "Organ of Montmartre Interests," explicitly formulating its territorial aspect—on the model of the animal whose name it borrows—while not hiding its imperialistic desire to make Montmartre "the center of the world."[1] It comes as no surprise, then, that an evaluation of the place of translated foreign literature in *Le Chat Noir* leads to the observation that it is quite rare, even almost nonexistent, including in the weekly bibliographical rubric that supposedly notes the latest publications. It is fitting besides to emphasize that some contributors active in the periodical, like Verlaine or Gabriel de Lautrec, did translate and publish foreign writers, more specifically English, but in other papers.[2] As for *La Vie Drôle*, gazette chatnoiresque, a spin-off of *Le Chat Noir*, launched by Allais and Auriol at the end of 1893 and powered by the fine staff from before 1893,[3] it resumes this editorial line, while keeping it to the scale of the paper, thus continuing the parodies of its predecessor. The aim of this chapter is to analyze the chatnoiresque attitude toward this proliferation of translations, and to observe to what extent this subversion allows it more broadly to ridicule the media field itself.

Translation: the Highlight of Modernism?

Let us return first to translation as seen by the writers of *Le Chat Noir*. For them, it is associated with school and with the past: it evokes above all the tiresome student exercise of Greek or Latin versions. Memories of school pepper the texts on this subject: "Et nous, nous végétons, à l'ancre / Dans l'encre / Et le Latin, égaux fléaux!"[4] [And we, we vegetate, at anchor / In ink / And in Latin, equal plagues!] It is in effect a rigid exercise, with an uncompromising solution, inasmuch as any departure from the norm is punished as an error. A story by Alphonse Allais[5] therefore presents a class's attempts to vary the translation that is expected, but predictable, repetitive, and ritualized, not to say foolish, by modernizing it, for the benefit of "interpretations that are audacious," because anachronistic, and which "provoke dull moans from their teacher":

"One fine day, in a Latin version, there appeared the word *onera,* the plural of *onus,* usually translated as 'burden.' This 'burden' began to irritate me. For a bit of a change, I translated it as 'baggage.' [...] *Puer* was constantly translated by Maurice as 'kid,' *lætitia* as 'fun,' and when we thought we had found in our version 'a courtesan of great beauty,' we could expect to read 'a very chic cocotte.'"

The method deteriorates, and a whole scale of variations becomes operative for the same Latin word: "Above all, poor *onus* did not escape. We had reached the point of using 'trunks,' 'suitcases,' 'packages,' etc." Even more than a refusal to take any discourse seriously, in reality the update critiques the fashion at the time for translating every text literally, word for word, at the risk of sacrificing its quality,[6] even of making it unintelligible.

This distancing from the original text, here evidence of indiscipline, also echoes a modality of translation in vogue at the end of the 19th century:

there is not only translation, there can also be adaptation, writing "after," or "free translation." This last genre of translation is, according to the statistics offered by the data base "Intraduction—Translation into French, 18th-19th centuries,"[7] in the period covering the appearance of *Le Chat Noir*, 1882-1897, very little used (only 3.4%). Although this analysis is only of titles published as books, and not in magazines, or even little magazines, it nevertheless indicates a tendency. Besides, this is precisely the genre principally chosen by the translators of *Le Chat Noir*. Not so much from concern for its rarity or for the marginal gesture, but because the name of the genre itself seems absurd, and probably affected. So it is "freely" that a story by Mather Smith is translated by Alphonse Allais;[8] hastily, in fact, because the original was published the same month in *Harper's Magazine*. Maurice Curnonsky uses a "rather free translation" of verses by "an ancestor of Leconte de Lisle," Lucrèce, as the comic ending of one of his articles,[9] by using the method of Allais's students. "Free": that epithet is then on everyone's lips, and is especially applied to all artistic innovation. Let us remember free verse, the quarrel over which is then raging among the literary set, or the Théâtre-Libre d'Antoine. Could "free translation" be the utmost in modernism? Its "highlight," according to the term of the times?

Perhaps, for after all, one might as well push it further, and proceed to the disruption of its codes in their entirety, from production to publication. Therefore the simple mention of "translation" is enough to signal the absurdity of the text to come, and to trigger a laugh. Alphonse Allais mocks this practice by annihilating the operation of translation itself, which consists of passing from one language to another. The syntagm "translated from," which constitutes the conventional peritextual apparatus, in order to clarify the text's original language, is distorted in "Poème morne—Traduit du suisse" [Sad poem—Translated from the Swiss].[10] Placed ironically under the aegis of negation—of all translation, therefore, but also of laughter, which is maintained throughout the text, beginning with the dedication to his humoristic colleague: "So that Auriol weep"—the poem assumes the defining features of the joke, that is, it "does not so much hide a presence as display an absence."[11] As with any good joke, Allais enjoys repeating it, notably when the text is published in a collection several years later:[12] "Poème morne" is then "translated from the Belgian." Such a mystification, organized in "complicity and exaggeration,"[13] because it is reserved for the readers of *Le Chat Noir*, recalls the provocative posture of the *fumiste* esthetic: "To make someone feel, in a large group, by a series of words, that he is an imbecile, is the nature of wit. To agree with him and hand him the very quintessence of his imbecility, is the nature of *fumisme*."[14]

Translation is consequently propelled into an interspace, between *fumiste* distancing and nuanced and subversive rearrangement, placing back-to-back conventional rigid academicism and the dullness of supposedly cosmopolitan translations produced by the avant-garde, to let the void spring forth.

Graecum est, non legitur

Because translating a text assumes making the original text comprehensible to the readership of another language, for the *Chat Noir* group it is a question of using translation to make it, precisely, unreadable. A way like any other to "turn the world upside down."[15] Not content with presenting dubious translations, *Le Chat Noir* enjoys jeopardizing all their possibilities of being read. There are, for example, announcements of forthcoming translations that do not exist, such as the *Contes du Chat Noir* [*Tales of the* Chat Noir] by Rodolphe Salis, supposedly translated into Russian at the request of the Emperor of Russia,[16] or the "translation of the telephone directory into Chinese, a work undertaken for some time…"[17] by a Henry Somm afflicted with "acute Japanism."[18] This last example tends to show how lacking in common sense a translator can be, in light of the absurd criteria guiding the choice of works he decides to translate. In *Le Chat Noir*, a text is sometimes published directly as a translation, even when it is the only version. This is the case with certain theatrical columns by Willy, one of which is written in a Greek of his own invention. The writer then plays on the delay caused by the replacement of each letter—or nearly—of the French text with its equivalent in the Greek alphabet:

Σάνς κὄντἔστέ ἶλ φαῦτ λοὔερ λ'εξ-Εδεν δε νοῦς δόννερ Lysistrata, πρίμο παρκε κὔε νότρε ἀμι Δόννη ρέγὄργέ δε τάλἔντ, πὺις παρκε κὔε σόν ἀριστόφάνεσκὔε φάντᾶσιε ἴνσπῖρα à Fernand Vanderem ὐνε πάγε ἐλοκὔέντε σὔρ λέ περε δες Φὄλλίκὔλαιρες κόμμε ἰλ λ'ἄππἔλλε.[19]

Beyond the exotic diversity of the languages invoked, we note the constant of linguistic choice: Russian, Chinese, Greek, that is, languages whose respective alphabets take hieroglyphic forms—in the eyes of the profane, or philistine. In the regime of mystification, their legibility is blurred. So much so that the reader, as we have detailed elsewhere,[20] invited to the party, must in turn put on a mask, that of a "*chatnoiresque* Oedipus,"[21] to decipher, divine, read between the lines. Or to read nothing at all, as seems to be emphasized by the last words of another of Willy's theatrical columns,[22] this time written entirely in Latin, "Graecum est, non legitur,"[23] by underlining the play on languages and history, reviving an expression borrowed from "ancient commentators or glossographers of civil law, who, not understanding Greek, passed over all the words in this language whenever they found them in their path, unable to explain them."[24] It is true that a hefty tome in Latin provokes an intense urge to leap over it, and never return. And the *chatnoiresque* convention of translating only for the sake of playing with the new rules within the literary field, all while amusing the gallery, seems to invite the reader to such a caprice…

Relying on his reputation as a humorist, as well as on the expectations of *Le Chat Noir's* readers, Willy finds a way to elude censorship in order to publish an article about *Lawn-Tennis*, the very controversial play by Gabriel Mourey, who was unable, for this reason, to have it performed in 1891 at the Théâtre-Libre, Antoine fearing a scandal—some scenes being considered too daring—that would have led to the closing of his theater.[25] This one-act play concerns in effect lesbianism in aristocratic circles, culminating in the strangulation of one of the protagonists by her mistress. Under cover of a foreign language, Willy takes a stand, in order to defend Mourey, because the affair is being debated in the press: he translates a passage from Antoine's letter of cancellation sent to Mourey at the last moment. Supplementary proof, if there ever was one, of the imposture of the famous epithet "free," on the part of of a theater that prides itself on innovation and audacity! And Willy seizes the opportunity thus given him to slip into his column a description of one of the lesbian scenes:

"Quaedum flebiliter effundit, insano quodam amore inflammata Camilla, invitam Helenam amplectitur, osculum osculo admovet, et cum singultibus, corpori corpus permiscet."[26]

The issue here, in a metalingustic way, is certainly that of subverting translation, that is, of manipulating the foreign language to make it indecent. *Una atque eadem opera aliquid facere!*[27] Inevitably, however, such an attack on morality is noticed by the defenders of the fin-de-siècle moral order, who seem not to have lost their Latin. To which Rodolphe Salis, the *gentilhomme-cabaretier* and editor of the paper, responds in an insert two weeks later, threatening to have *Le Chat Noir* appear "in Latin, even in Arabic, if that does not suffice," if "those gentlemen of the public prosecutor's office" still dare to "object to our way of having fun."[28]

Despite the resort to a dead language, here the mechanisms of literary modernity are laid bare. By muddying the waters, it is a matter of the group assuming a *fumiste* position. In effect, we are no longer sure if *Le Chat Noir* is denouncing an imposture, by turning translation into a hoax, or adhering to the practice by reinvesting it, and in so doing, renewing it, by presenting a group ready to make a distinctive brand of it. However, whether couched as a (false) engagement, a joke, or a threat, the *chatnoiresque* translation is systematically late in coming. More precisely, this temporal distancing of translation becomes a system. It is part of the joke, but also sets itself against the flow of the quasi-industrial production rate of translations—which it means to critique—focusing on their appearances in periodicals. Taking liberties with a translation that will never appear, repeated excuses for this delay, and excuses for the author's procrastination as well, all renew and reinforce the *fumiste* posture par excellence.

A Parody of the Media Circulation of Translations

The subversion of translation takes on a new dimension in *La Vie Drôle, gazette chatnoiresque*. This periodical whose existence is brief—only eleven weekly issues—is also a playing field that its authors claim as more experimental than *Le Chat Noir* had been, in the declared intention of distancing itself from it. A hoax is therefore conducted from issue to issue. The gazette never stops promising the reader a fabulous serial that will come to its columns, *Le Roi des Madrépores* [The King of the Madrepores], and this without ever mentioning the author, although it could be guessed—Alphonse Allais—the title being the name of Captain Cap's boat.[29] Conducted with the heavy use of advertisements, to the point of ingeniously interfering with the format of the paper, by interrupting a story or serving as an interlude between two texts, a text finally does appear, which is not the one that was expected: *Le Roi des Madrépores* will never be published in *La Vie Drôle*—nor elsewhere. This text, ironically entitled "La Verité sur *Le Roi des Madrépores*"[30] [The Truth About *The King of the Madrepores*], explains the editorial conditions that led to the delayed publication of the gazette's star serial.

Let us summarize. Seeming much like an adventure novel—which in fact is what we were promised[31]—the story retraces the fantastic story of the theft of the manuscript by a certain John Flip, who translates it into English and then burns the original manuscript, before traveling around the world to try to sell it to the most established anglophone papers: the *Times, Harper's Magazine*, the *Sydney Herald*, and the *Sydney Daily News*, all willing, apparently, to pay a fortune for it. But the correspondents of *La Vie Drôle*, on the alert, try to stop the translator. Recovered just before its publication in an Australian periodical by W. G. Stevenson, correspondent for the *Sydney Daily News*, the translated manuscript is finally returned—by ship, which delays even a little longer its reception in France—to the staff of the paper that owns it exclusively. In order to read this novel that the whole world is trying to obtain, we must first await its translation back into its original language.

The joke might seem anecdotal, especially when published in a periodical that is equally so, if it did not condense single-handedly all the failings of the virality of translation, as well as the inner workings of the media field and its artifices, which the authors of *Le Chat Noir* endlessly display and distort. In fact, Allais is unable to deliver his text on time, due to a certain aptitude for procrastination, as well as a sojourn far from Paris and his journalistic activities.[32] It remains striking that he resorts precisely to the subject of translation as an excuse. Efficiently presented, the story stages in a literal way the circulation of media thwarted by unpredictability. A circulation that, normally, exceeds the cadre of little magazines. All of the elements specific to the publication of translations in periodicals are heavily mobilized, such as the possibility of reproducing a text in a great number of issues, its ruthless translation, its economic value, the questions of literary property, and the connections between journalists at a henceforth international scale, all by means of correspondents. Pretending to an international network and exaggerating the interest in its productions, *La Vie Drôle* moves backwards on this fully expanding field.

In doing so, Allais torpedoes the opposition between cosmopolitanism and nationalism, as relayed by the press.[33] It is by no means a question of knowing if a text in English would be unpublishable in France, and inversely. The geographical modalities, here stretched to the breaking point, as well as the pertinent linguistic impasses, are reversed to the benefit of the temporal paradigm, all equally binding in the media regime. If the translation of *Le Roi des Madrépores* is late in coming, it is no longer Allais's responsibility: he passes the buck to two collaborators on *La Vie Drôle*, Paul Fabre and Maurice O'Reilly,[34] "sworn translators of M. T. B. S." Translation? *Mean Time Between Sorties*, perhaps.

In a dynamic of both avant-gardism and differentiation, the subversion of translation is as good a way as any to address a practice then agitating the literary and media field. Although parody is very significant at the end of the 19th century, particularly in *Le Chat Noir*, which makes it a principle of writing, parody specifically pertaining to translation and its codes seems more marginal. The texts discussed here are not only chosen examples; they constitute all in all a micro-corpus within the paper, which warrants examination. They have however allowed us to reveal an alternative position to cosmopolitanism, as disparaged at the time by nationalists. Rather than attack, *Le Chat Noir* sidesteps the issue: it bypasses the debate animating the literary and media field in the 1890s, and defuses it by constant discrepancies. These writers take a malicious pleasure in, on one hand, overshadowing translations of modern languages (English, for example) by preferring dead languages, and on the other hand, proposing their own "modernist" versions by fanciful treatments, with the help of linguistic blunders and dissociations between the stated and the statement. With this properly *fumiste* employment of the distancing of the text, the target is simultaneously more global and more difficult to discern. It is more precisely the dominant institutions, which at the same time practice translation and diffuse its productions—school, literature, the press, the field of performance—that are intended. By this reflexive approach, a marginal gesture in the fin-de-siècle press, *Le Chat Noir* nevertheless raises real questions about the practice of translation, its codes and its status, and in that, no doubt involuntarily, is ahead of its contemporaries. Finally, we witness a theme treated in an episodic fashion in the history of the periodical that interests us. After the massive defection of the editorial board of 1893, and its initial repatriation in *La Vie Drôle*, the editorial policy of *Le Chat Noir* abandons subversion across the board, to turn toward "good French song," at the very moment that we witness an "important restructuring of the literary field that could be summed up by the term 'transnationalization'"[35] after 1895. By dint of procrastination and playing hooky, *Le Chat Noir* missed jumping on the bandwagon!

CHAPTER SIX

"Killing oneself to amuse others,"[1] or the mechanisms of suicide for laughs

Judging by the obituaries and homages to artists in *Le Chat Noir*, death carries off a number of them between 1882 and 1897. There are many causes, but no suicides![2]

Yet this is how it all begins at *Le Chat Noir*: Rodolphe Salis, the *gentilhomme-cabaretier*, was supposedly unable to bear the fact that Émile Zola had stolen his idea to write *Pot-Bouille* [Pot Luck], thereby preventing him from attaining the rank of "national poet,"[3] and sent a bullet into his brain. On April 22, 1882, on the front page of the paper, there appears an obituary, inviting readers, artists, and family to the wake; here is how it went:

"The shutters closed, the room draped in black and lit by candles, a 'cello on a trestle, covered in black serge, represented the catafalque, next to which kneels the painter Signac, dressed as a nun. A skull is placed on a chair. The sprinkler for washing glasses lay in a basin filled with water, and, to the astonished arrivals, Deschaumes, costumed as the master of ceremonies, ordered coldly, 'Spray!'"[4]

The singers Jules Jouy and Maurice Mac-Nab noisily accompany the ceremony; as for Émile Goudeau, he recites the Pater Noster. To conclude this macabre party, Salis arrives in person to thank everyone for the splendid funeral they have just offered him.[5]

In keeping with the *Chat Noir* artists' penchant for provocation, bad taste, and mystification, the suicide is a joke, just like the wake: it is a question above all of promoting the cabaret. The objective is attained: it is the talk of Parisian society. And Vingtcholle makes light of it in "À ceux qui bavent sur un cadavre"[6] [To those who drool on a corpse]. Various articles in the press, no doubt fake, are listed. Journalists are said to have taken the opportunity to speak poorly of *Le Chat Noir* and Salis, notably M. Wolf, the famous editor of *Le Figaro*, who evokes a "pasteboard glory": "If he thinks he held an important position in my time, he is mistaken, I tell him this frankly, although he is no more."

Beyond the aspects of entertainment given this event, there is a remarkable paradox: a suicide, by definition an individual act, is staged and orchestrated collectively, to bring better and louder laughter. We therefore propose to investigate the original place of suicide in the paper; its coordination with the foolish and collective *chatnoiresque* humor seems, from issue to issue, like a joke repeated and improved in the same circles, to create cohesion within the group.

"Let Us Suicide Them!"[7]

In the fin-de-siècle context still marked by the Commune and, above all, by joyous and uproarious cabaret, suicide can only be mocked in the paper's texts and illustrations. To hang oneself, why not, but "temporarily, on the pretty necks"[8] of young ladies. In effect, in *Le Chat Noir*, they are in favor of life and its pleasures:

> Pourvu que notre corps supporte sans souffrance
> Les rires et le vin, la joie et l'espérance,
> Volontiers nous existerons.[9]

> [Provided that our body can withstand without suffering
> Laughter and wine, joy and hope,
> Willingly shall we live.]

"Brother, one must live!"[10] becomes their rallying cry, which is echoed in Émile Goudeau's commentary on the subject of *Parce, Domine, Parce, populo tuo* by Adolphe Willette (1884), which decorates one of the walls in the cabaret: "Brother, one must turn away in time!"[11] The painting shows in effect a whirlwind of vices—women, money, pride—driving Pierrot to suicide, recalling the "danger of growing old in bohemia."[12]

Moreover, these artists consider suicide a motif belonging to a bygone literary past:

> La Mort qui nous étale
> Avant le couvre-feu
> Est une horizontale
> Vieux jeu.[13]

[Death that lays us out
Before the curfew
Is an old-fashioned
Whore.]

To mock it becomes henceforth a way to critique inspiration and the literary style of past writers, and therefore organizes the cohesion of a group that wants to be both singular and innovative.

At first it is Romanticism that is targeted. The motif of suicide satisfies the quest for elevation, infinity, and eternity proper to the movement. The obsessive aspect of this fascination with death and with the act that brings it has a corollary, in *Le Chat Noir*, in the systemization of references to the best known Romantic works. For example, some of their titles are incorporated into the texts. The title of Alfred de Musset's famous novel[14] thus serves as a schematic periphrasis to designate a young suicide: "a child of the century";[15] the title alone of a collection by Victor Hugo[16] provides the punchline for a very short poem by Andhré Joyeux:[17]

Regards, œillades, frôlements,
Baisers, caresses, délire,
Collages, dèche, embêtements,
Suicide!…—Toute la lyre!

[Looks, winks, touches,
Kisses, caresses, frenzy,
Clinging, poverty, troubles,
Suicide!…—The whole lyre!]

These verses crudely summarize Romantic amorous lyricism in which passion leads to suicide, and, reciprocally, suicide proves passion. The height of the passionate impulse residing in suicide between lovers is therefore subverted into the pinnacle of stupidity in "Suicide en partie double"[18] [Double-entry suicide] by Maurice Mac-Nab:

Mourons ensemble
Pour être heureux;
La mort rassemble
Les amoureux!

C'est demain matin qu'on se noie
(Faut-il qu'un amour soit profond!):
Je ferai la planche avec joie
Pendant qu'elle ira boire au fond!…

[Let us die together
To be happy;
Death brings together
Lovers!

Tomorrow morning we shall drown ourselves
(A love must be deep!);
I shall float on my back with joy
While she goes for a drink at the bottom!…]

The abandonment of this commonplace is represented here by the male lover's detachment: this half-missed suicide lets him happily rid himself of a lover he finds too mawkish.

Short work is also made of "spleen," a late and acute relic of Romantic discontent. The first verse of Charles Baudelaire's fourth "Spleen"[19] is taken literally in an (apocryphal) eponymous poem parodistically signed by Juliette Lenbaire—a joke, incidentally, targeting the very serious Juliette Lambert. Scorning metaphysical melancholy, the lyrical subject fantasizes about a more definitive "crushing":

Oh! Par ce temps de plomb, ce ciel outrecuidant
Où le spleen semble avoir promené sa palette
Je sens éclore en moi le désir obsédant
—D'être écrasée par l'omnibus de la Villette.[20]

[Oh! In this leaden weather, this arrogant sky
Where spleen seems to have used its palette
I feel blossoming in me the obsessive desire
—To be run over by the La Villette bus.]

Furthermore, Baudelairean black humor is reconfigured according to the *chatnoiresque* codes. The cabaret context counters it with a variation in green absinthe. So, in "Sonnet morne"[21] [Gloomy sonnet] by Jean Richepin, suicidal thoughts give way to drunkenness, and moans change into a hiccup that is sounded ironically by the dieresis on the word "suicide":

Mais on est lâche; on se décide
À retarder le suicide;
On lit; on baille; on fait des vers;

On écoute, en buvant des litres,
La pluie avec ses ongles verts
Battre la charge sur les vitres.

[But one is cowardly; one decides
To put off suicide;
One reads; one yawns; one makes verses;

One listens, while drinking beer,
To the rain with its green fingernails
Sound the charge against the windows.]

The gamut of black liquids also undergoes declension: bile is subverted into excrement. The song "L'Anderlique de Landerneau ou le Préjugé triomphant (Légende bretonne)"[22] [The Tub of Landerneau or The Triumph of Prejudice (Breton legend)] by André Gill thus tells the story of a rejected cesspool worker who makes his full barrel the method and place of his suicide:

L'vidangeur, la mort dans l'âme,
Sentit qu'par les préjugés
De ce pèr' vraiment infâme,
Ses jours d'vaient être abrégés…
Ouvrit sa bonbonnière
Où l'espace paraissait noir,
Et, la tête la première,
S'y jeta de désespoir…

Destinée mélancolique,
Cet amant eut pour tombeau
L'anderlique, l'anderlique,
L'anderlique de Landerneau!

[The cesspool worker, death in his soul,
Felt that because of the prejudices
Of this truly vile father,
His days must be shortened…
Opened up his barrel,

74

Where the space seemed black,
And, head first,
Threw himself in from despair…

Melancholy destiny,
This lover had for a tomb
The tub, the tub,
The tub of Landerneau!]

This suicide serves above all as a pretext for the exemplification of the binomial *colique/mélancolique*, a cliché they never tire of in *Le Chat Noir*,[23] and which, incidentally, plays on Hugo's definition of puns, those "droppings of the mind."

But it is not only the writers of the past that are parodied: their contemporary peers, especially the Decadents, also are. In effect, these last base their esthetic on an escape from the horror and triviality of existence. Their pronounced taste for nothingness and decay, as well as the emphasis on individuality,[24] lead to making the suicide an emblematic figure. "Le suicide du décadent"[25] by Paul Rey suggests this inescapable link by an alliteration ironically close to a tongue twister: "le décadent décida de se suicider" [the Decadent decided on suicide]. Although the suicides in Decadent literature have the merit of being original, it is precisely that quest for the rare, bordering on somewhat sophisticated refinement, that is mocked. C. G. Konan exaggerates the point by turning a suicide by hanging into a moment saturated with previously unknown sensations, and consequently even more voluptuous and exquisite:

"First a soft murmuring buzzed in his ears, as muffled as the sound of distant waves breaking on a cliff, then a splash seized him […]. His eyes opened. The air then seemed striped with thin bands of rosy pink flickering around a golden halo.

"The slow agony was ending; short vibrations shook the swinging body, vibrating to the sobs with which Death caressed his nerves, like a piano. For an instant, his flesh shivered at the contact with the dead woman's flesh, […] and the long shadow of his hanging body was outlined in black on the dark drapery of the curtains."[26]

It is also the Decadent style that they seek to profane. The esthetic pleasure of resorting to rare terms is overturned by the systematic use of hackneyed qualifiers, and the accumulation of precious terms is subverted into pleonasm. This is how Charles Leroy tells the story of the suicide of a tapeworm escaping from its late proprietor's corpse—it is in effect pursued by the undertakers:

"Now worn out, the tapeworm finds an open door and seeks refuge, exhausted it seeks a hiding place, and commits suicide itself to escape certain death, by diving headlong into the first hole that it finds."[27]

The statement in the margin of the text is displayed: the process of decipherment and the reader's horizon of expectation are laid bare and incorporated into the text, before being dismantled. The existential ennui that leads to suicide is converted into lassitude for the traditional treatment of this cliché. Rather than expiring, one only sighs when faced with this decidedly overused topos: "Cut your carotid / With a razor, razor."[28] Its use is therefore modified. It is no longer a question of revealing personal neuroses, but of seducing an audience with plays on words, references, intertextual allusions, that only the group can understand and enjoy at their true value. To increase the effect, the artists of *Le Chat Noir* add their own grain of salt: the *fumiste* laugh.

Cum grano [S]alis

The *fumiste* posture evokes a suicide for laughs: it comes back to "sawing off the branch you're sitting on, for fun."[29] It's as good a way as any to "turn the world upside down,"[30] a world in which suicide evokes a laugh that is ambivalent and foolish, and, even better, irrepressible. Laughter therefore shakes the bodies of suicides, like Cleopatra "smiling—as if tickled by legless serpents."[31] The strings of the comic are reinvested. Suicides arrive in droves, imitating the comedy of repetition: there are thus multiple attempts at suicide—four times (defenestration, drowning, bullet to the head, second defenestration) in "Le Roman d'un Peintre"[32] [The Novel of a Painter] by Steinlen—but which fail every time, or two simultaneous suicides over the body of a man who has just been murdered.[33] The excess of this specific laugh bursts upon our ears by the onomatopoeia that augments the descriptions. So, those who throw themselves in the Seine make a "plouff!"[34] whereas pistol shots go "crac!" As in "La Ballade des Camélias" by George Auriol: "He pulls from his pocket a small ivory object. The object goes crac! and the man sways on the carpet like a puppet whose strings have been cut. He falls and goes pouff!"[35]

The motif of suicide takes up, more broadly, the defining characteristics of the joke. Following the etymology of the word,[36] suicide swings between too full and empty, simultaneously. The artists of *Le Chat Noir* proceed by a "crude and childish schematization,"[37] that is, they push the cliché of suicide toward the grotesque, by means of hyperbolic treatment. That most often turns the treatment bizarre and contradictory, triggering the laugh. If with Maurice Rollinat, in "Mademoiselle Squelette"[38] [Miss Skeleton], everything is reduced, the suicide "si maigrelette" [so teeny-tiny], resorting to a "cordelette" [little string], with Alphonse Allais the hanged man uses "a long rope, so very long!" to the point of letting a bawdy meaning swell up in the text:

"And the next day, when, before the mayor of the village, they cut him down, an unbelievable number of people, in accordance with his last wish, were able to share the interminable rope, and it was for all of them an infinite source of lasting happiness."[39]

Like the hoax involving Salis, suicide as treated in *Le Chat Noir* is by nature just as ludic as deceptive. It is not by chance that the false suicide took place in April. The first of April, the day for jokes par excellence, is, in effect, a privileged moment to end one's days, or at least to pretend to. In a wordless picture story by Dōes, "Termes d'avril"[40] [April rent], the character pretends to commit suicide to avoid paying his rent: with his sheets and pillows, he imitates the body of a hanged man, before running away. The language itself participates in the act of undermining. The expression *faire un poisson d'avril* [make an April fish, that is, fool] is depicted in a concrete way:

"In the first days of April [...] he sent into space a heartbreaking adieu, threw himself with a leap into the river, and... since he was an excellent swimmer, he landed on the opposite bank."[41]

This phrase also resemanticizes the designation of the suicide's body in "Espérance"[42] [Hope], by Raphaël Shoomard: "For a moment, as a fish wiggles at the end of a line, he struggled with great convulsive arching of the back..." By means of this abundantly developed metaphor, it is the screwball *chatnoiresque* art that is shaken under the reader's nose. Let us remember in fact these verses from Charles Cros's "Hareng saur" [Salt Herring]:

Et, depuis, le hareng saur—sec, sec, sec,
Au bout de cette ficelle—longue, longue, longue,
Très lentement se balance—toujours, toujours, toujours.[43]

[And since then, the salt herring—dry, dry, dry,
At the end of that string—long, long, long,
Has been swinging very slowly—forever, forever, forever.]

Because of this mystification pushed to the utmost, disguises are exchanged, categories unravel, leading to a "generalized indistinctness"[44] that is strictly *fumiste*. So, what we think is a suicide is not, as in "Premiers froids"[45] [First Frost] by Alphonse Allais: the hanged man and the woman who "shot herself with a revolver" are in fact two wax dummies that their owner, a "former showman who earned a considerable sum by showing famous crimes in wax," takes out to his garden "to avoid mold." And, inversely, what is not *a priori* a suicide ends up resembling one. In Jules Jouy's "Pantomimes-express—II L'Aéronaute"[46] [Instant Pantomimes—II The Balloonist], for example, Pierrot, "in an aerial captain's uniform," finds himself in a balloon that "tumbles from the sky." He tries to drop some ballast, in every way: undressing, cutting his nails, shaving, blowing his nose, vomiting—but he hasn't eaten—all in vain. In so doing, the writer propels the reader beyond common sense, drawing the statement out to the point of absurdity:

"… The balloon keeps falling; it will crash to the ground! A brilliant idea illuminates the aerophile's brain: he rids himself successively of all his limbs and throws them from the nacelle. When he reaches the ground, he has neither head, arms, legs, nor torso. But he is unharmed."

By scuttling in this way the methods and codes of suicide, it is the joke itself that falls flat and elicits a failed laugh, much like the "failed mayonnaise that spurts from the cranial vault"[47] of someone who shoots himself in the head. In the paper *Le Chat Noir*, one commits suicide, just as one bursts out laughing, "for nothing."[48] So, a young student in a story by Alphonse Allais "finds nothing better to do than to hang himself, just to put on a brave face."[49] All these methods of suicide—cutting the carotid, shooting oneself, jumping in a "hole,"[50] opening up the belly, drowning ("that makes rings in the water"[51])—depict the violence done to common sense and, in addition, recall the collective pleasure of exploring the void. The joke about suicide thus represents the exchanges, centripetal and ephemeral, of the *chatnoiresque* group.

Suicide: A Good Collective Joke

In *Le Chat Noir*, art is lived and practiced collectively. A very pronounced intertextuality connects the texts and illustrations, and is organized "in complicity and exaggeration."[52] One of Paul Lheureux's aphorisms—"a soap bubble bursts, we inflate another"[53] underlines that, collectively, the same gag is inflated. The joke about suicide has a very *chatnoiresque* nature, it would have even more than nine lives: it is made to die again and again.

Imitating the commonplace of suicide is conceived as a linguistic and entertaining performance, joining the pragmatic aspect proper to the cadre of cabaret. The text, like the body, is dislocated by "side-splitting" puns that aim above all for laughter among peers. So in "Sur la pendaison et les avantages qu'elle procure"[54] [On hanging and the advantages it provides], by Em. Moreau-Verneuil, we hear between the lines the poet getting tipsy on the feat of assembling so many ways of evoking hanging:

Ce gai (!) Marseillais —l'homme «dernier cri»—
Qui chez Duclerc «daigna» se pendre,
Aura *jusqu'au bout* tenu son pari…
Il va de l' «au-delà» descendre.

Du clocher voisin, minuit lentement
Se décroche… Voici qu'expire.
Au treizième jour, le dernier moment
De cette pendaison pour rire (?…)

[…]

Peut-être «essaierai-je» un jour, *cependant!*
Oui, pour (après une harangue
À mes créanciers—ce sera *tordant!*)
À la Guigne tirer la langue…

[This merry (!) Marseillais—the "fashionable" man
Who at Duclerc's "deigned" to hang himself
Will have upheld the bargain *up to the end*,
He will descend from the beyond.

From a nearby bell tower, midnight slowly
Falls… Here it is expiring.
On the thirteenth day, the last moment
Of this hanging for laughs (?…)

[…]

Perhaps "I shall try" one day, *however!* [with a pun on *pendant*,
hanging]
Yes, in order to (after a harangue
To my creditors—that will be *hilarious!*) [with a pun on *tordant*,
twisting]
Stick out my tongue at Bad Luck…]

In addition, a mechanism of this variation can be observed. Thus writers try to come up with the stupidest or most ridiculous suicide. Maurice Rollinat, a regular in the early days of *Le Chat Noir*, publishes "Le Magasin des suicides" [The Suicide Store] in his collection *Les Névroses*[55] [*Neuroses*]:

Nous avons l'arme à feu, le rasoir très coupant,
Le foudre à bon marché, l'asphyxiant chimique

[We have firearms, very sharp razors,
Cheap powder, chemical asphyxiant]s

The idea of making suicide one's business is taken up again in a story by George Auriol, "La Fête des morts"[56] [The Feast of the Dead]. The hero walks by the large stores, among them a "General Contractor for Suicides." Later, Ticket in "La joie de Deibler"[57] [Deibler's Joy] modifies this paradigm by applying it to a very large model of razor: a guillotine blade. The choice is enough to satisfy any client:

PURCHASE AND SALE OF USED IMPLEMENTS
Repairs and exchanges
Lessons in assembly and disassembly.—Special classes for ladies.
RENTALS FOR SUICIDES
Better bargain than the revolver.—Try and compare!

We make special implements to order, depending on the case:
A heated guillotine for clients with delicate lungs.
A ground-floor guillotine for rheumatics who cannot climb the steps.
A guillotine with a padded lunette, for sensitive throats.
A guillotine in tempered steel for rainy regions.

On the model of the *fumiste* laugh, which is indirect, and even "reflected once, twice, often ten times,"[58] the joke only takes effect later, in an "unexpected"[59] way. It is in effect by these games of resonance, acting like a collective work in progress, that it grows from issue to issue. And this, to the point of making the *Chat Noir* artists themselves part of it, by incorporating them into each other's jokes. George Auriol thus makes Jules Jouy the main character in "La guillotine fatale."[60] This man is a singular suicide because he chooses the guillotine: he calls himself "born for the scaffold." To be certain of achieving his plans, he murders his maid. Beyond the comic content of the story, Auriol here makes a reference to the works of his friend, a singer whose repertory is so stocked with this subject[61] that his contemporaries call it an "obsession."[62] This idée fixe is taken literally and constitutes the punchline of the story: Jouy's autopsy reveals that "HIS BRAIN [...] HAD THE TRIANGULAR SHAPE OF A GUILLOTINE BLADE!" Mélandri, on his part, reclaims the facetious Alphonse Allais. In "Hara-Kiri,"[63] a parody of the novel of that name by Harry Alis,[64] another participant in the cabaret, the famous humorist appears as a coroner.[65] His final "reasoned" diagnosis is as ridiculous as his stories published in the paper: the Prince of Japan, from whom he extracts among other things "an exotic sword 75 centimeters long," which he had driven into himself, "died from a stomach ache." Finally the *Chat Noir* itself comes into play, as in Willette's "Pierrot s'amuse"[66] [Pierrot has fun]:

"Pierrot goes mad and adores the moon. Pierrette, still looking for him, finally finds him, but hanging from a streetlamp, she weeps.

"Pierrot hanged!!!!!

"The Black Cat eats a mouse ....
...."

By means of the suspension points, the joke continues although the text ends, its range carrying above and beyond the absurd. *Le Chat Noir*, collectively, could not care less about the hanged man. What is important to the artists is making their colleagues laugh, probably at the expense of morality. By these variable and sinuous movements of connection, the group embraces a careless and free understanding of the world, outside the limited stability of official writers, outside established genres and conventional thought.

In a dynamic of avant-gardism and differentiation, the subversion of suicide, that threadbare cliché, is obligatory. By dangling before the reader the disarticulation of this commonplace, the *Chat Noir* artists touch upon everything that makes up established art and its crude common sense. The *fumiste* stunt of Salis's suicide shows the performative aspect given it from then on: it is reinvested to depict this sociability in the eyes of the world. Although this act, individual by definition, is redirected into a ritual practice aiming to show the group in its unicity, we can add that it leaves the private sphere and contaminates not only the contributors to the paper, but the readers or spectators, who are also provoked, taken to task, appealed to.

However, this is not to everyone's taste, including those who attend the cabaret. An article by Jules Vallès, "Aux copains du *Chat Noir*"[67] [To the friends of *Le Chat Noir*], thus appears in the columns of *Le Chat Noir*—proving these artists' propensity to laugh also at themselves:

"Above your art, there is the social question.

"Above your Louis XIII cabaret, there is the church of the Sacré-Coeur that grows larger on your skulls.

"May the thought that is within it explode like a mine, sending sanguinolent pieces of Jesus to the Devil.

"The hour has come when all ideas must be cutting—like swords.

"In this red and stormy air, in which the next revolts are rumbling, the attitude of 'who cares?' could not survive.

"Friend Salis, move then, to see, your beer cart to the banks of the great yellow Seine.

"It will be strange indeed if your poets do not feel blowing through their hair a wind of anger as they listen to the voice of the river, that walking cemetery, as Pascal would have said.

"One evening, I predict, the verses, music, and brushes will stop, stricken by the final cry of a suicide!"

PART 3:

EMBODYING POETIC ECCENTRICITY

CHAPTER SEVEN

Eroticism...

LE CHAT NOIR

Le Printemps, par André GILL

VIVE LA RÉPUBLIQUE.
ÇA POUSSE!

Pornographic. This is the qualifier the paper finds attached to it from the very beginning, as reported in an editorial note in the tenth issue.[1] To which André Gill maliciously responds, in the same issue, with a full-page cartoon showing a pubescent Marianne feeling her exposed breast, and captioned: "Long live the Republic! It's growing!"[2] Although the law of July 1881 proclaims freedom of the press, thereby hindering censorship and allowing the written press to grow in importance, a second law, passed in August 1882, focuses exclusively on the question of affronts to public decency, with readers seen as victims. The period covered by the appearance of the paper coincides with that of greater moralization in society, mostly concerning nudity, equated with pornography. This does not fail to be mentioned in succeeding issues. There are consequently three powerful government officials who are targeted, Félix Ravaisson, Frédéric Passy, and René Bérenger, who in effect have worked to remove nudity from the public sphere. Not satisfied with multiplying legislative strategies against it, and forming leagues, like one against licentiousness in the streets—or in "rutting," as Raphaël Shoomard points out, punning on *rues* and *ruts*[3]— these men pursue nudity even in academic art—and not only in magazines sold at kiosks—even though it had been offered for contemplation since antiquity. Shown to be well established in this way, since it is displayed in the form of statuary in public parks and other sculptures on the facades of official buildings—think of allegories of the Republic, for example— it is a matter of limiting it. There is thus an attempt to cover genitals to hide them from view. *Le Chat Noir* takes a malicious pleasure in reporting this news by exaggeration, making these curators—of the department of antiquities at the Louvre[4] for Ravaisson, and of the moral order for Passy and Bérenger—pathetic profaners. These "Princes of the Fig Leaf"[5] thus make themselves noisily noticed in numerous texts and illustrations. In a story by George Auriol, Ravaisson, appropriately called "Vine Blossom"[6]

because he wants to put them "on Watteau, on Phidias…"[7] finds himself accused, by Jules Grévy in person, of having tried to infect the statues in the Louvre "with the indecent phylloxera,"[8] for which he is punished. As for Frédéric Passy, he, made up as an "abominable gnome,"[9] behaves, despite his advanced age—the cause of the "suffocating odor of rotten eggs that infests the street"[10] at his passage—like a street urchin, and goes every evening to throw mud at the Diane by Houdon that adorns the hallway of the cabaret. As for Bérenger, even his shadow ironically takes the shape of a fig leaf in "Scandale à l'Opéra"[11] by Gabriel Amoretti. This wordless picture story shows the characters from Carpeaux's *La Danse*—the nudes in the scandalous statue that adorns the facade of the Opéra Garnier—free themselves from their base to join the festivities and fully incarnate the allegory they represent, before being called to order by Bérenger, who commands them to return to their pedestal. That is, to remain in the only domain that is, despite many reservations, conceded to them. In fact, this story evokes a very real scandal, that of the Bal des Quat'z'Arts, and joins the *chatnoiresque* initiative to defend their friends and colleagues. A lawsuit for affront to public decency is in effect filed by René Bérenger, the well named "Père la Pudeur" [Father Prudery], senator and president of the "Ligue de la Défense de la Morale," against models who have appeared in the nude. And among them Sarah Brown, playing Cleopatra "lying on a palanquin and carried by a half dozen handsome fellows dressed as Egyptians."[12] A method adopted, then, to remove art from its own domain, to bring images to life and integrate them into society: it is the time of the first pictorial performances.[13] "At any rate," for Alphonse Allais, "it was much prettier than if they had carted around Jules Simon or Frédéric Passy in the same costume."[14] Beyond mocking the conservatives' position, *Le Chat Noir* tends to show how much they lack common sense. And even though, following this position taken in favor of the Quat'z'Arts, the paper finds itself censored by a zealous printer,[15] these artists will never think of taking back the "mots très crus, / Nus, / Drus"[16] [very raw, / Naked, / Strong words] that fall from their pens.

In fact, nudes are displayed in the pages of the paper. Sometimes in close-up. Bawdy stories and erotic poems are also plentiful. We shall cite particularly two signed by Edmond Haraucourt, who published the famous *Légende des Sexes—Poèmes hystériques* [Legend of the Sexes—Hysterical Poems] (1883)[17]. But the expression of nudity could not be reduced to that of the body, the woman's in particular, in a paper devoted to syllepsis.[18] Besides, what could be better, to baffle censorship, than to defer the representation of the nude toward a cosmic, ideal, divine, beyond: *nues* also means "sky"! Far from simply taking back Romantic poetry for themselves, the poets of *Le Chat Noir* superimpose their enormous laugh on the universal macrocosm. One of them even makes it his specialty: Jean Rameau. Which his *chatnoiresque* colleagues do not fail to underline in their reviews of him, while multiplying their praises of his undeniable poetic inspiration. Stanislas de Guaita, in an article on his latest collection, *La Vie et La Mort* [Life and Death], thus evokes a lyricism that is "broad […], powerful […], of exuberant force,"[19] and another evokes the "vertigo of the infinite"[20] caused by reading his verses, resting on an "imagination infatuated with grandiose conceptions."[21] For, in fact, Rameau's lyricism is extravagant and cosmic. His powerful poetic inspiration leads him to flirt sometimes with the stars,[22] sometimes with the sun,[23] and even to approach the seventh heaven by "fucking a planet":

> Et tout m'aimait, et tout s'offrait, charnel, avide;
> Et mon cœur aimait tout d'un amour de tempête
> Comme si fauvement j'étais, dans le ciel vide,
> Un grand soleil de chair baisant une planète.[24]

> [And everything loved me, and everything offered itself, carnal, eager;
> And my heart loved everything with the love of a tempest
> As if I wildly were, in the empty sky,
> A great sun of flesh fucking a planet.]

The decor of the cabaret brings other elements meant to display the group's insistence on preserving its artistic and ideological liberty. We cannot speak of erotic decoration; but one figure stands out and recurs like a leitmotiv in the paintings, stained glass windows, and objects that adorn the cabaret, and did so since its beginning. This is the virgin, on whom we shall linger further. Making use of her might appear paradoxical; yet, she is emblematic of bohemian life, expressing a quest for the ideal that becomes implacably corrupted, despite all efforts; there is also an ironic allusion to a century in which virginity possesses social value, against a background of religion that sets it up as the supreme value. Willette, the painter who collaborated regularly on *Le Chat Noir* at the paper's beginning, contributed to the emphasis on this figure, conceived as an antagonist to the *Chat Noir*—in its various meanings—because of her mythical whiteness, to which we shall return, but also to the neighborhood in which the cabaret was located, Montmartre, then known for welcoming many houses of prostitution, relegated to the outskirts of Paris. Thus, *La Vierge au Chat* [The Virgin with Cat], also known as *Vierge Verte* [Green Virgin], oil on canvas (1882), which served as the model for the stained glass window of the same name that will adorn the first floor of the second cabaret (1885), shows a fully dressed young woman—in a long green dress and high collar—a lily wrapped around her waist, raising an aggressive black cat above her head, both haloed by the moon behind them. There is also the "chorus of virgins" visible on the lower right of his gigantic canvas *Parce Domine, Parce populo tuo* (1884); as Phillip Dennis Cate stresses, this depiction of "free-loving artists and dancers floating above central Paris is a complicated, macabre narrative relating the loss of sexual and moral innocence incurred by the decadent life in Montmartre engendered by the *Chat Noir*."[25] Finally, as we mentioned earlier, Rodolphe Salis installs, by the entrance to the second *Chat Noir* cabaret, a statue of Diana, which is a copy of Houdon's *Diane* (1776), the virginal goddess.

The figure of the virgin, and the clichés surrounding her, in particular the moment of defloration, is also a topical figure of erotic literature, which, as subversive by nature as it is, cannot escape the parodistic transgressions and misappropriations that the artists and writers of *Le Chat Noir* made their specialty. The pages of the paper abound in dramatizations of that unique and ephemeral moment par excellence that is defloration—the height of the casual affair, characteristic of bohemian life—expressed in ambivalent and absurd ways, simultaneously cruel and jubilant, offensive and mystical.

The intangible codes surrounding this motif—an intact hymen, the purity resulting from moral innocence—are reworked and reutilized in a literal way, and coarsened. Thus, the virgin is a condensation of purity: "impeccable virgin [...] / Pious and chaste,"[26] and her hymen takes on exaggerated dimensions, both in size—in Edmond Haraucourt's "Le Cloître-Sonnet"[27] [The Convent-Sonnet], it takes the form of a white veil worn by the young women—and in thickness: it is compared to a "drumhead" in Haraucourt's "La Vieille"[28] [The Old Woman]. In accordance with the games of excess in *Le Chat Noir*, virgins are sometimes very young children,[29] but also, in contrast, women so old they are close to death, as in Haraucourt's "La Vieille," which presents a scene of masturbation:

Dans l'âpre isolement de sa couche dernière,
Crispant ses membres secs sous ses rideaux en deuil,
Elle bave d'amour en attendant sa bière…

[In the bitter isolation of her last bed,
Tensing her thin limbs under her mourning drapes,
She drools of love while awaiting her bier…]

88

Innocence is varied according to its etymology: *candeur* means "whiteness." The virgin's body is superlatively white: "Whiter than sheer satin,"[30] "Whiter than candle wax."[31] These descriptions also echo, parodistically, Gautier's "Symphonie en blanc majeur" [Symphony in white major], in which "women-swans" have "skin whiter / Than the snow of their down." This whiteness, absolute and extravagant, invades the space of the text or illustration, like one of Alphonse Allais's monochromes, completely white, entitled *Première communion de jeunes filles chlorotiques par un temps de neige* [First communion of chlorotic girls in snowy weather] (1883), and which can turn, as Maurice Rollinat stresses in the poem "La Virginité,"[32] into a "white nightmare." To link purity to a negative vocabulary in this way leads to inexorable corruption, which Louis Denise[33] expresses as "perverse virginities" and "unhealthy virgins." This oxymoronic aspect is also found in slang, since *blanchisseuse* [laundress] means "prostitute," specifically "fellatrix," derived from *blanc*, money or sperm.[34] On the model of the snow that it exemplifies, virginal purity, being ephemeral, can only be dirtied:

Au contact du Paris boueux,
Sceptique, étrange et monstrueux
Qui déflore toutes les vierges.[35]

[At the touch of muddy Paris,
Skeptical, strange, and monstrous,
Which deflowers all virgins.]

So that white turns into other colors. First of all, red, the expected color. "La Virginité"[36] by Maurice Rollinat enumerates the "blushes" of the virgin, simultaneously the "confession" of her prerequisite virginity, by the cliché of shedding blood, and the revelation of the pleasure she feels: she blushes in pleasure. This fantasy about the virgin's pleasure is abundantly dramatized, expressed in Haraucourt by the dehiscence of her "flower": "And the flower of her nubility, / Purple, blossoms under the baptismal wave!"[37] But red also provokes a shift to the macabre. So, in "Sur le vif"[38] [From Life] by Alphonse Allais, the forced undressing of a "very young" woman escalates into her skinning, the skin seeming like an extension of the thin membrane of the hymen:

"The rajah stood up straight, as if mad, and roared: 'More!'

"The poor little dancing girl, terrified, instinctively checks with her hands to see if she forgot some fabric, around her body

"But no, she is quite naked.

"[…] He roars again: 'More!'

"They have understood.

"The large knives leave their sheaths.

"The servants skillfully strip the skin from the dancing girl.

"And soon she appears before the amazed rajah like an anatomical specimen, gasping and steaming.

"And the rajah is no longer bored."

Specifically, Allais amuses himself here by dramatizing concretely the bawdy slang expressions concerning coitus or the male sex, which are usually overlaid with images of white weapons: saber, dagger… The artists of *Le Chat Noir* reinvest this tradition, while demystifying it and even updating it: the revolver—which additionally means "a good lover" in slang—succeeds the traditional implements.[39]

Other colors, less expected, result from a reshuffling in line with the *chatnoiresque* color scale: green and black. Green, although traditionally associated with raw eroticism, veers, in *Le Chat Noir*, toward parody. For example, the "Symphonie en blanc majeur" by Théophile Gautier (from *Émaux et Camées* [*Enamels and Cameos*]), mentioned above, becomes, under the pen of Georges Vicaire and Henri Beauclair, a "Symphonie en vert mineur (Variations sur un thème vert pomme)"[40] [Symphony in green minor (Variations on an apple-green theme)]. Thus, in Willette's stained glass window *Te Deum laudamus*,[41] placed on the ground floor of the second cabaret, green and black wind around the white body of a young virgin. A black cat—representing the *Chat Noir* group—throws itself at the surprised woman's neck; although she tries to protect her flower, a white lily, which she holds at arm's length, the green background leaves no doubt about the deflowering to come. As for black, besides its association with the cat, it also symbolizes ink. In effect, the whiteness of the virginal body is a metaphor for the white page, which in turn attracts the obsessive desires of the poet, as in "Ballade à la Lune"[42] [Ballad to the Moon] by Numa Blès: "White, much more than the banal lily and banal ermine! White that would be the envy of the angelic wings that we suppose!" So that the practice of writing takes on the trappings of the erotic act, mimicked by its comings and goings, allusions to legs or to the first night of a virgin,[43] the pen,[44] and all the verbs that suggest coitus:[45]

"The whiteness of the paper is fascinating. The pen sets off, the pen walks. It runs. At first, there are regular lines, oh! all inspired. Downstrokes that are straight, slender, elegant.—He heats up; the lines broaden, the downstrokes lengthen.—He pulls himself together; thick and violent deletions spread across the page.—His pen takes off again; it runs again.—How the whiteness of the paper is fascinating!"

"Romance" by Ferdinand Loviot spins out the metaphor, by tinging it with occultism:

Ton âme est une page blanche
Dont, tôt, la griffe du Malin
—Vers elle qui déjà se penche—,
Ternira, d'un geste vilain,
Le pur et précieux vélin…[46]

[Your soul is a white page
Where, soon, the claw of the Evil One
—Which already bends toward it—
Will darken, in an ugly gesture,
The pure and precious vellum…]

However, the writers of *Le Chat Noir* do not only exaggerate the clichés of erotic literature, they stretch the phenomenon of defloration to the point of absurdity. After having enumerated the various representations, all very visual, given to virginity, we shall observe the more unexpected way in which they turn to sonic effects, to mimic society's propensity for making such a loud noise about the loss of virginity.

Although on paper noises can only be imagined by the reader, erotic literature opens up a wide range of expected sounds: sighs, moans, speech going out of control, wilder until the final orgasm, as in "Sonnet pointu"[47] [Sharp Sonnet] by Edmond Haraucourt, for example; as soon as there is a question of defloration, words are replaced by cries and tears, due to the pain that is part of the clichéd description of the moment. *Le Chat Noir*, however, seems to realize that something is missing. In fact, since medical discourse conceives the hymen as a membrane that tears, its loss must be sonic. The writers therefore focus on this sound. Charles Cros resorts to the clichéd metaphor of the lily, by juxtaposing it with the Latin etymology of "defloration"—*defloratio* meaning the action of withering a flower: "Let us crumple those lilies!" he calls out in "Vertige"[48] [Vertigo]. As for Haraucourt, he speaks of "explosion",[49] in another poem, "La Vieille"[50] [The Old Woman], precisely because of the late loss of virginity, and the fantasy of a thick-skinned hymen, he evokes a loud sound: "And her virginity of antique parchment / Cracks like the skin of an old drum when it bursts." Since there is sound, wordplay based on sonic effects abounds. This is particularly the case with the pun, based on homophony. Thus, "Variations sur l'amant d'Oline"[51] [Variations on Oline's lover] by Gaston Parsac is constructed around a pun, ringing out the word *choc* [shock], representing the loss of virginity:

Après un bal chez la Marquise,
Lorsque l'aube apparaît exquise
Dans la splendeur de son éclat,
Colas, reconduisant Oline
Offrit—de sa voix fort câline—
Le chocolat.

Puis, dans la chambre de la belle,
Qui pour lui se montra rebelle,
Il fut très tendre, mais hélas!
Malgré le feu sacré de l'âme,
Il ne put assouvir sa flamme
Le chaud Colas.

Car Oline, étant encor sage
Voulait défendre son… corsage
Et refusait fort bien—cela,
Disant: «Je t'aime bien, sans doute,
Mon adoré, mais je redoute
Le choc—Holà!

[After a ball at the Marquise's house,
As dawn breaks, exquisite
In the splendor of its brightness,
Colas, seeing Oline home,
Offered—in his quite caressing voice—
Chocolate.

Then, in the room of the beauty,
Who proved resistant to him,
He was very tender, but alas!
Despite the sacred fire in his soul,
He could not quench his flame,
The hot Colas.

For Oline, being still good,
Wanted to defend her… blouse,
And refused—that— quite firmly,
Saying: "I like you, without a doubt,
My adored one, but I fear
The shock—Stop!"]

Paradoxically, although Oline's virginity is saved, the pun reorients the meaning of the poem, so that the only thing that breaks is laughter, "ambiguous and blurred."[52]

Besides, in the pages of *Le Chat Noir*, it is precisely laughter that replaces the expected cries and sighs—the analogy is all the easier since it too is not articulated like language. Thus, the young women depicted in erotic texts burst into laughter,[53] whether before, during, or after their deflowering. Like pleasure, it passes through the entire body, up to the face, whose features it distorts. Laughter transforms exhilaration, in that it arrives to complete it, as in "Sonnet—Les lits"[54] [Sonnet—Beds] by Félix Décori:

Puis, après les soupirs, les râles et les fièvres,
Quand le sommeil unit les lutteurs apaisés,
Un rire inachevé voltige sur leurs lèvres.

[Then, after the sighs, groans, and fevers,
When sleep unites the sated wrestlers,
An unfinished laugh flutters on their lips.]

In fact, although Pierre Guiraud reports in his *Dictionnaire historique, stylistique, rhétorique, étymologique de la littérature érotique* that the word *rire* is given the meaning *coïter*,[55] the laughter emanating from the virgin's body takes it into an updated representation. Charles Cros, in his story "Le Caillou mort d'amour"[56] [The Lovesick Pebble], presents in a way that is dystopian, but eminently symbolic, the courtship of a flint—himself a virgin—for a crevice "produced in the virgin soil" of the moon. When the flint stops "hard, straight, stupid," before Augustine (that being the name of the crevice), the latter's laughter is described as "modern," and proceeds, in an explicit and provocative manner, to an invitation to go further:
"The crevice burst into a delicious, but silent, laugh, peculiar to the Beings of the Planet with no atmosphere. Her features, in this laugh, far from losing their grace, gained an indefinable quality of exquisite modernity. Larger, but more coquettish, she seemed to be saying to the pebble: 'Come on then, if you dare!…'"

Although the virgin, modernized, laughs, even silently, the noise around her deflowering continues none the less to resonate, and like a joke, is amplified in the columns of *Le Chat Noir*.

It is in effect a question of mimicking the collective attention paid by all segments of society—religion, medicine, etc.—and pushing it to the point of absurdity. The writers thus critique the foolishness of this common logic by raising unexpected questions. This is the case for example with Edmond

Haraucourt, who wonders about the future of post-defloration virginities in his Villonesque "Ballade des pucelaiges morts"[57] [Ballad of dead virginities]:

> Sont-ils eslus, ou damnés malement?
> Quel aultre monde assemble leurs collèges?
> Le Ciel o luz, ou l'Enfer o torment?
> Mais qui Dieu sçait où vont les pucelaiges?

> [Are they saved, or cruelly damned?
> What other world reunites their assemblies?
> Heaven with its light, or Hell with its torment?
> But who for God's sake knows where virginities go?]

This reflection, with its mystico-philosophical trappings, quickly assumes a dramatic tone, the speaker feigning compassion for this empty entity, underlining in effect the violent death that every hymen suffers, in a vision that is moreover egalitarian:

> De Royne, nonne, ou ruste mal facée;
> Estroit ou lé, Lorrain, Bret ou Flamand,
> Trestous, occis par l'espoux ou l'amant,
> De mesme mort meurent sans privileges

> [Of queen, nun, or ill-favored peasant;
> Tight or wide, from Lorraine, Brittany, or Flanders,
> All, killed by the husband or lover,
> Die the same death, without privileges.]

Other writers, for their part, dramatize the pretext of the medical examination that verifies the hymen is well and truly intact. Because it touches on the profoundest intimacy, the contrary is presented by making public demonstrations of it. A text by Dubut de Laforest, "Les Vierges contemporaines"[58] [Contemporary Virgins], thus depicts this type of examination, in the form of a contest that awards first prize to "the one who *is* the most of all…" In addition, the scientific aspect of such an act is also subverted, since it is practiced by "the inventor of a system that allows him to evaluate exactly and mathematically the degree of virginity." For, as the main character points out, virginity can be measured, but still keeps its enigmatic trappings, about which even a scientist can only speculate, particularly since the object of his research seems to be on the road to disappearance:

"Where does virginity begin?… Where does it end?… The ancients, notably Horace and Propertius, mention some young women who do not even remember having been virgins. Bold commentators have gone so far as to claim that the institution of our contests was becoming useless, virginity having become exiled from this earth […]"

The figure of the virgin is far from being a Muse of *Le Chat Noir*. In light of the statues that adorn the streets, nude but immobile, and which *Le Chat Noir* nevertheless shows in the act of dancing, she incarnates the willingness of the group to metamorphose matter, to put "flesh in revolt," as it comes to "claim its rights,"[59] as Haraucourt puts it, to validate the "creative spasm"[60] which, alone, must command the act of writing.

CHAPTER EIGHT

Chamber Pots, Enemas, and Cannulas

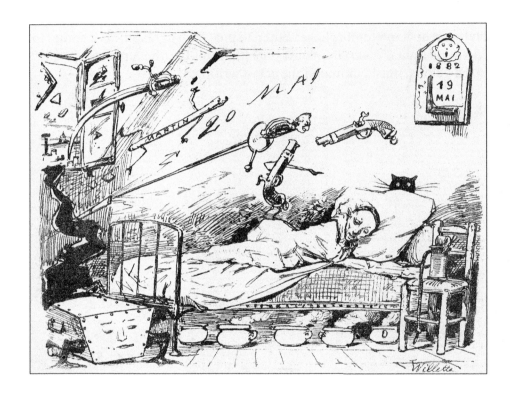

At the end of the nineteenth century, the relationship with ordure is different from ours. Indeed, domestic and personal toilets are rare; the visual and olfactory fields, private as well as public, are therefore occupied with the matter. Whereas on one side hygienists, driven by bourgeois propriety and growing industrialization, wage battles for urban as well as corporal purification, on the other, cartoonists and men of letters, among others in the "little" marginal magazines of the avant-garde, continue to mock the practices of a society seen as absurd and stinking. In effect, the command for generalized restraint does not seem to have affected the more immaterial domains, such as the literature appreciated by the middle class—naturalistic and realistic novels, in particular those borrowing the proper sentiments—to the great annoyance of Léon Bloy, notably. He therefore writes in the columns of *Le Chat Noir*:

"If someone like M. Ohnet or M. Paul Alexis, for example, said: 'My heart is a chamber pot so full that the smallest drop of the ink of criticism makes it overflow,' he would express with astonishing energy, at once both the truth of his own case, and the general state of French hearts at the end of the nineteenth century. [...] What emerges from these *vases* on our boulevards is unbelievable. Once they're jostled, the vile contents leap out with all their perfume, and this is, in short, the very exact configuration or literary analysis of all contemporary *emotion*.

"There is an eye at the bottom of those vases."[1]

The critic shows his visceral refusal of the intimate as a psychological or sentimental given, a far too tenacious residue of a Romantic nineteenth century. Whereas material ordure is henceforth destined to be cleaned up and sorted, this is not however the case with that which, to him, is as dubious as it is repugnant: the "overflowing"[2] of the *self*.

Although Bloy's remarks are usually considered violent, including by his collaborators at *Le Chat Noir*, in this particular case these last share not only the bias, but the form: collectively, the intimate is taken literally, in its grossly material sense. Besides, it is not dictionaries that will say the contrary. Derived from the superlative *intimus*, the term thus refers back etymologically to what is "most internal." The *Trésor de la langue française* [*Treasury of the French Language*] reports its different meanings in this way:

"What constitutes the fundamental traits proper to a given individual, his essential nature; what is connected to the most personal in him.

"That which is the most profound, the most essential, the most original in a person.

"What favors the blossoming of profound internal life, meditation, by its isolation, its quiet calm."[3]

The definitions already include simultaneously the ideas of profundity, blossoming, interiority, and necessary isolation: they combine on their own the characteristics linked to scatology. The artists of *Le Chat Noir* do nothing but rework them, all while demystifying, exaggerating, and playing with them. Thus conceived, the intimate is displaced from its conventional support. It deviates from a dubious and empty self, and therefore projects onto the exterior, onto the surface, what should come from interiority. We cannot however speak of objectivity, but rather a dedramaticization of everything connected to the intimate sphere. It therefore seems more appropriate to speak of effects of objectification, that is of a staging of the process "by which an internal state is projected onto the exterior."[4] It is a question of projecting an interiority, whether it be vacant or congested and not hierarchical, onto external elements, in this case objects. Chamber pots, enemas, and cannulas distort the expected depiction of intimacy by exaggerating and displaying it. Beyond its entertaining aspect, the presence of scatological objects in the texts as well as illustrations seems at the service of a critique concerning the dysfunctions that touch the writers of *Le Chat Noir* even more intimately: the connection with poetic creation.

An Intimate Bond Between Characters and Their Chamber Pots

The connection with the object is pre-eminent at the end of the nineteenth century, not only because of the bourgeois society that exhibits what it owns in showcases, and of capitalism, but of the Decadent estheticism that displays an often luxurious decor: the object defines the intimate space. At *Le Chat Noir*, this fault of the period is stricken with deviation. An intimate connection certainly appears between subject and object, but on condition that the latter be a chamber pot. From a utilitarian object with a precise function, it becomes the useless object par excellence, and with no real function other than decorative: a bibelot. The fin-de-siècle taste for this type of materiality becomes reinvested: that which is used to disencumber the interior of the human body then encumbers the characters' interiors, and is even collected. Therefore piles of chamber pots and commodes are described or drawn. An untitled drawing signed by Saint-Maurice[5] shows objects classed by size, by type, according to whim, mimicking the visual pleasure of the collector—which is, besides, what distinguishes a collection from mere bric-a-brac. We can count nine of them: a commode, two barrels, two slop pails, two chamber pots, and two portable urinals. Amusing fact: George Auriol dedicates to Rodolphe Salis one of his stories,[6] which recounts a man's obsession for buying chairs of all kinds, among them commodes—he owns four of them. We should recall that the *Chat Noir* cabaret is described by its regulars as "a sort of temple of the bibelot":[7] Salis himself is struck with "collectomania"; he creates a decor made up of bits and pieces "in disorder."[8] To this systematic accumulation of objects, of a sometimes serial character, the *Chat Noir* artists oppose the accumulation of similar objects. In a drawing by Willette,[9] we therefore see "Pierrot colique, Pierrot fichu"[10] [Colicky Pierrot, wretched Pierrot], in bed, an Éguisier irrigator on a chair; under the bed, since that is the traditional place, is not just one chamber pot, but five, identical, all similarly fuming.

The inverse process is equally recurrent: the bibelot is made into a chamber pot. More precisely, it is the bourgeois bibelot, that is, an object used for organizing smaller objects, or foodstuffs not necessary for existence, that is appropriated in this way. So, in a tale by Rodolphe Salis,[11] the punchline depends on the protagonist falling into the village's *fientoir* [Old French for "shithole"], renamed for the occasion *Drageoir aux Cholliques*. The two objects have in fact a similar form: a *drageoir* [box for dragées] is also a "vase with raised edges."[12] Although we can imagine a possible nod to *Le Drageoir aux épices* [*The Box of Spices*] by Joris-Karl Huysmans (1874), it refers more to the slang treatment of the language of confectionery, another element common to these two objects.[13] In point of fact, it is the periphrastic way to designate fecal matter in slang: chestnuts,[14] prunes,[15] pralines…[16] It is also a question, in another of Salis's stories, of a "cake of excrement"[17] into which the protagonist falls. The contents consequently follow the metaphor: *drageoir*, but also *bonbonnière*[18] [candy box or septic barrel]. The song "L'Anderlique de Landerneau ou le Préjugé triomphant (Légende bretonne)"[19] [The Tub of Landerneau, or The Triumph of Prejudice (Breton

Legend)], by André Gill, thus tells the story of a rejected cesspool worker who makes his full barrel the method and place of his suicide; to do this, he "[o]uvrit sa bonbonnière / Où l'espac' paraissait noir." [opened up his barrel / Where the space seemed black]. Finally, still in slang, another form of the word *drageoires*[20] means "cheeks," more precisely those of the buttocks.

Furthermore, the fashion is then for Chinese and Japanese bibelots. From the Chinese porcelain vase to the chamber pot is only a step, which is taken by Émile Goudeau by exaggerating it. "Sonnet Extrême-Orient"[21] therefore depicts two Asians in the act of defecating:

Ka-Ka-Doi, mandarin militaire, et Ku-Ku,
Auteur d'un million et quelques hémistiches,
Causent en javanais sur le bord des potiches,
Monosyllabiquement d'un air très convaincu.

Vers l'an cent mil et trois, ces magots ont vécu
À Nangazaki qui vend des cheveux postiches:
C'étaient d'honnêtes gens qui portaient des fétiches
Sérieux; mais, hélas! chacun d'eux fut cocu.

Comment leur supposer des âmes frénétiques?
Et quel sujet poussa ces poussahs lymphatiques
À se mettre en colère, un soir? Je ne sais pas!

Mais un duel s'ensuivit.—Ô rages insensées!
Car ils se sont ouvert le ventre avec fracas
Voilà pourquoi vos deux potiches sont cassées.

[Ka-Ka-Doi, military mandarin, and Ku-Ku,
Author of a thousand and some hemistichs,
Chat in Javanese on the edge of vases,
Monosyllabically with great conviction.

Around the year one hundred thousand and three, these dwarves lived
In Nagasaki, that sells artificial hair:
They were honest men who carried serious
Fetishes: but alas! Each was a cuckold.

How can we imagine them with frenzied souls?
And what subject drove these lymphatic roly-polies

To become so angry, one evening? I don't know!

But a duel ensued.—Oh insane rages!
For they opened each other's bellies with a crash.
That is why your two vases are broken.]

Goudeau plays on Sully Prudhomme's "Vase brisé" [Broken Vase] differently than by pastiche—there is even a question of *postiches*. Here, the lyric subject denies all responsibility for being the cause of the "crash" of the "vases" belonging to the lyric addressee, thus inverting the postulate of the hypotext. To do this, he invents a story based equally on intimacy, except that this one appears shifted off-center, toward the lower body. As is attested by the wordplay and obscene sounds that punctuate the sonnet. The act of evacuation in effect slips into the phonic material of the words. Rather than opening himself up intimately, the "I," here, gives his personal and imaginative vision of a small and trivial domestic event.

Not as trivial as that, really: this poem metaphorizes on its own the typical *chatnoiresque* treatment. Whereas the carnivalesque tries to overturn order,[22] the artists of *Le Chat Noir*, "in complicity and exaggeration,"[23] aim at putting everything in disorder. It is a question in fact of disrupting intimacy and, simultaneously, clouding the issue, creating confusion. On contact with the excremental, the categories of objects crumble, and this following a logic that is seemingly implacable: if chamber pots and bibelots become indistinguishably the same object, consequently any object can receive the material.

Unseemly Projections

Following the example of the collector who accumulates objects as rare as they are strange, to assemble and arrange them in a cabinet of curiosities, the *chatnoiresque* shitter shows a certain taste for heterogeneous "places." There are therefore an umbrella,[24] a screen in his hosts' bedroom,[25] "from the knees to the codpiece"[26] of his pants, his future coffin,[27] or, more metaphorically, death, as in "Philosophie—*Sonnet honteux*"[28] [Philosophy—Shameful sonnet] by Edmond Haraucourt:

C'est la Vie: on s'y jette, éperdu, puis on tombe;
Et l'Orgue intestinal souffle un adieu distrait
Sur ce vase de nuit qu'on appelle la tombe.

[That's Life: we plunge into it, distraught, then we fall;
And the intestinal Organ breathes an absent-minded adieu
On this chamber pot we call the tomb.]

These stories are not devoid of echoes of contemporary social and technical advances: although, still in the nineteenth century, "the 'all-in-the-street' remains the law of housewives, despite the risk of its translation before the police court,"[29] various decrees of urban sanitization aim for the definitive end of this custom. One of the traditional comic devices, projection of excrement and sprinkling by urine, is thus on its way to going out of style. The artists of *Le Chat Noir* leap at this windfall, while following the fashionable logic of keeping all one's personal effects at home: that which is no longer spread in the streets and on passersby will henceforth be found in the intimate sphere of the room, preferably spattering the face of the pharmacist or physician. They mock in this way even society's frenzy for purgation. Indeed, although cleaning the streets is important, keeping one's interior clean is a weekly preoccupation: purgative waters, such as Sedlitz or Hunyadi-Janos, lozenges, teas, enemas, and cannulas are all used, and promise to restore a "fresh and rosy color,"[30] "perfect health,"[31] a sentiment of the Ideal. Athanase, an apprentice apothecary in a story by Alphonse Allais,[32] pays the price as he gives a patient an enema:

"There was nothing left but to withdraw it and to leave.

"But suddenly, like a volcano, like an explosion, an unexpected phenomenon occurred.

"Projected violently outward, the good liquid was just leaving [...]

"Athanase's face was right there, in point-blank range. He didn't miss a drop."

A wordless picture story by Fernand Fau[33] widens the field of projection. One therefore sees a young patient in bed receive an enema from her doctor; the splattering happens immediately, falling not only on the doctor, but on her father and the maid, who falls backwards.

Laughing at everything, but especially at themselves, the artists of *Le Chat Noir* do not confine themselves to showing the absurdity of society by provocations, they equally attack the dysfunctions that affect fin-de-siècle creation, more precisely poetry.

Intimate Visions

Victor Hugo summarized it in these sententious words: "Poetry is everything that is intimate in everything."[34] It is consequently not surprising that this genre be more profoundly targeted in *Le Chat Noir*: the poets denounce the pretenses of such a conception. In "L'Œil"[35] [The Eye] by Armand Masson, the different meanings of the word "eye" refer to each other, in other words, a *trompe-l'œil* appears beneath the surface. Thus, Fifine must overcome her fear of the eye "adorned with a violet eyebrow / And a pupil painted in bright red" found at the bottom of her chamber pot, so that her own eye can open:

L'œil était dans le vase. Un caprice d'artiste
L'avait agrémenté d'un sourcil violet
Et sa prunelle peinte en rouge vif semblait
Vous regarder d'un air ineffablement triste.

C'est à la Foire aux pain d'épices qu'un beau soir
Nous gagnâmes ce vase au tourniquet, Fifine.
Affirma qu'il était en porcelaine fine,
Et voulut l'étrenner tout de suite, pour voir.

Mais il était si neuf, le soir, à la lumière,
Qu'elle n'osa ternir sa pureté première,
Et le remit en place avec recueillement.

Elle fut très longtemps à s'y faire. C'est bête:
Cet œil qui la fixait inexorablement
Semblait l'intimider de son regard honnête.

[The eye was in the vase. An artist's caprice
Had adorned it with a violet eyebrow,
And its pupil painted in bright red seemed
To look at you with an ineffably sad expression.

It was at the Gingerbread Fair one fine evening
That we won this vase at the spinner. Fifine
Claimed that it was of fine porcelain,
And wanted to try it out immediately, to see.

103

But it was so new, that evening, in the light,
That she didn't dare sully its first purity,
And reverently returned it to its place.

She took a long time to get used to it. It's stupid:
That eye that stared inexorably at her
Seemed to intimidate her with its honest gaze.]

For, if "there is an eye at the bottom of those vases,"[36] as Léon Bloy writes, it is certainly the poet's. The *Dictionnaire Larousse* defines the intimate as "that which is the most profound of something, which constitutes the essence of something and remains generally hidden, secret." The poet's function, since Romanticism, has been precisely to decrypt the signs: "he sees,"[37] writes Victor Hugo; he is the "decipherer [...] of the *universal analogy*"[38] for Baudelaire; Rimbaud makes him a "*Seer*."[39] This principle is subverted, in *Le Chat Noir*: it is the intimate object that inspires the "I"-poet's vision. Furthermore, the object in question has a precise and unique function: an enema, or any object related to it. It is a question, then, for the "I," of a contact with intimacy, not his own, but the other's—the woman's—by means of their respective anatomical parts, with a similar name: the eye. This is the object that is the link between them.

The game is certainly not new. We can think of certain pictures that show amorous scenes, like *Le Clystère ou la Soubrette officieuse* [*The Clyster or the Obliging Maid*], an engraving by Alexandre Chaponnier, after Schall (1786): the enema is used as a pretext to show her intimate parts to her lover-voyeur, hidden behind the door of the room. The enema, a syringe, thus becomes tinged with an erotic function; some even call it the "joyous syringe."[40] But, in *Le Chat Noir*, this is once more exaggerated, all the more so because it permits them to touch on the function of the "I"-poet. In "Seringue-Pompadour"[41] by Armand Masson, the lyric subject devours the said object with his eyes:

Svelte et luisante, elle repose
Sur un coussinet de velours,
Dans un coffret en bois de rose
Portant l'écusson aux Trois Tours

C'était l'exécutrice intime
Des ordonnances de Quesnoy

Elle présidait au régime
De la confidente du Roy;

Et sa prison capitonnée
D'étoffe bleue aux tons éteints
Conserve une odeur surannée
Où revivent les jours lointains.

Ce miracle d'orfèvrerie
Est en vieil argent ciselé
Où la galante mièvrerie
De ce siècle du potelé

Mit une ronde fantaisiste
D'anges aux derrières joufflus,
Qui semblent courir à la piste
Des appâts qu'ils ont entrevus.

—Oh ! s'ils pouvaient parler, ces anges
Si par leur voix m'étaient contés
Les souvenirs des lieux étranges
Qu'ils ont autrefois visités;

Si la gloire était révélée
De tous les charmes inconnus
—Où la seringue fuselée
Déposa ses baisers pointus...

Sur leur beauté mystérieuse
Nous aurions des détails précis
Et pour l'Histoire curieuse,
Bien des points seraient éclaircis ;

Nous verrions sous une autre face
Ce chef-d'œuvre cythéréen
Qui tenait alors tant de place
Dans le concert européen ;

Et, dans une auréole exquise.
Paraîtrait aux yeux éblouis
Ce que la divine marquise

Gardait aux plaisirs de Louis.

Or, c'est dans l'espérance intime
De connaître un jour ce secret
Qu'un pharmacien que j'estime
Conserve ce bijou discret;

Car c'est pour lui comme un emblème
De ce privilège ancien
Qui laissait au pharmacien
Le plaisir d'opérer lui-même.

[Slim and glistening, it lies
Upon a little velvet cushion,
In a rosewood box
Bearing the crest of the Three Towers.

It was the intimate executrix
Of Quesnoy's prescriptions.
It presided over the diet
Of the King's confidante;

And its padded prison
Of blue cloth with faded tones
Retains a musty odor
Where distant days live again.

This miracle of metalwork
Is of old chiseled silver,
Where the amorous sentimentality
Of that plump century

Placed a fantastic ring
Of angels with plump derrières,
Who seem to chase after
The charms they have glimpsed.

—-Oh! If they could only speak, those angels,
If in their voices I were told
Memories of the strange places
They visited long ago;

If the glory were revealed
Of all those unknown charms
—Where the tapered syringe
Planted its pointed kisses…

About their mysterious beauty
We would have precise details,
And for curious History,
Many points would be clarified;

We would see under another face
This Cytherean masterpiece
Which then held such a position
In European accord;

And in an exquisite halo
There would appear before our dazzled eyes
That which the divine marquise
Kept for Louis's pleasure.

Now, it is in the private hope
Of learning this secret some day
That a pharmacist whom I esteem
Keeps this discreet jewel;

For to him it is like an emblem
Of that old privilege
That left to the pharmacist
The pleasure of operation himself.]

The meticulous observation of this finely crafted and worked object, kept in a case just as luxurious, gives it the aspect of a fetishized object, even of a relic; it also reveals the obsession accorded this object, as much by the "pharmacist"[42] as by the "I," even if the latter only appears furtively. Through its intervention, the contemplator penetrates the intimacy of a fantasized woman, even more so since she belongs to "distant days," and pierces her mysteries. The lady's sphincter seems to have turned into a *fumiste* variation of the sphinx, bearer of a "secret" that will never be revealed. Consequently, by both the object and the fantastical projections it inspires, the observer's eye tries to see something else, to perceive the beyond. But this is reduced: it is only the woman's anus. The contemplator's eye then replaces the fantasized eye.

"Le Clysopompe"[43] [The Clyster-Pump] by Maurice Mac-Nab makes the "I" intervene even further. At first a voyeur, the subject fantasizes himself as an injection-pump, another instrument used for enemas, combining a syringe, a tube, and a pump that allows a continuous stream. The lexical field of sight acts as a connective thread, and thereby allows the "I" to draw closer to the lady:

> N'auriez-vous pu, madame, à mes regards cacher
> L'objet dont vous ornez votre chambre à coucher.
> Je suis observateur, et, si je ne me trompe,
> Le bijou dont je parle était un clysopompe!
>
> Jamais on n'avait vu pareil irrigateur!
> Orné d'un élégant tuyau jaculatoire,
> Vers le ciel il tendait sa canule d'ivoire.
> Spectacle sans égal pour l'œil d'un amateur!
>
> Sur la table de nuit dans l'ombre et le mystère,
> Sans doute il attendait votre prochain clystère…
> Mais qu'importe si j'ai d'un regard indiscret
> De vos ablutions pénétré le secret!
>
> Ce qu'il faut vous conter, c'est que la nuit suivante
> Un cauchemar affreux me remplit d'épouvante:
> J'ai rêvé… que j'étais clysopompe à mon tour,
> De vos soins assidus entouré nuit et jour.
>
> Vous me plongiez soudain au fond d'une cuvette,
> Vous pressiez mon ressort d'une main inquiète,
> Sans vous douter, hélas! que votre individu
> Contre mes yeux n'était nullement défendu.
>
> Et moi je savourais l'horizon grandiose
> Que je devais, madame, à ma métamorphose.
> Si bien qu'en m'éveillant je m'étais convaincu
> D'avoir toute la nuit contemplé votre…

[You could not, madame, have hidden from my sight

The object with which you adorn your bedroom.
I am observant, and, if eye am not mistaken,
The jewel of which I speak was a clyster-pump!

Never had such an irrigator been seen!
Adorned with an elegant projecting tube,
Toward heaven it stretched its ivory cannula,
A spectacle without equal to the eye of a connoisseur!

On the bedside table in shadow and mystery,
No doubt it awaited your next enema…
But what does it matter if with one indiscreet look
I penetrated the secret of your ablutions!

What I must tell you, is that the following night
A dreadful nightmare filled me with terror:
I dreamed… that I was a clyster-pump in turn,
Surrounded by your constant care night and day.

You plunged me suddenly deep into a basin,
You pushed my spring with a worried hand,
Without suspecting, alas! that your person
Was in no way forbidden to my eyes.

And I savored the grandiose horizon
That I owed to my metamorphosis,
So well that on waking, I was convinced
That all night I had contemplated your…]

Here the fantasy is tinged with the fantastical, and makes us, in trompe-l'oeil, believe a nightmare. The different meanings of the word "I" overlap, contaminating one another, on the model of a subject-voyeur who confuses himself with an object dedicated to dispensing an enema. The vision, itself multiple, both sense and imaginary mental representation, acts as an intimate link between the disparate elements. Finally, the "I" sees just as much as he has given himself to see. Having become a "jewel" belonging to a fantasized feminine display, he can be placed beside the other intimate bibelots already cited. The access to a vision beyond the sensory world that is traditionally reserved for the poet, although seemingly denied to the *chatnoiresque* "I"-poet, is metamorphosed in turn: these are visions, with variations that are just as extended; at least, as far as the meaning and sonorities of a word can allow.

Making chamber pots, enemas, and cannulas the crucible of fin-de-siecle intimacy might seem a provocation that is at best bold, at worst in bad taste; particularly since these objects offer nothing new in the matter of social or political satire, and even seem to be obligatory references. However, more than a fin-de-siècle reappropriation of the carnivalesque, which notably manifests as a reversal of hierarchies and therefore favors the "productive lower body,"[44] it touches on more intimate subjects than it seems. Under the deceptive "externals" of a literal conception of intimacy, it is a question for these artists of giving their personal, although collective, vision, against the background of the fin-de-siècle crisis of the ideal, of poetic dysfunction. Although the connection with the "intimate" object tends by definition and by social obligation to be individual, it is diverted by these artists into a ritual practice aiming to show the group in its unicity and to look at social and poetic practices from a shared viewpoint.

CHAPTER NINE

"Let Us Be Fine Chiselers of Turds?"[1]: On the Art of Making Well

Intempestive Substitution, par Does.

To the tune of "Cadet Rousselle":
"Ah! Ah! c'est révoltant
Ce que Paris est dégoûtant!"[2]
[Ah! Ah! It's revolting
How disgusting Paris is!]

In this fin-de-siècle period, hygienism, the doctrine barring the unclean from the sight, sound, and smell of society, is succeeded by therapeutic hygiene: one must also be clean internally. Purging oneself becomes a weekly preoccupation:[3] purgative waters, such as Sedlitz or Hunyadi-Janos, lozenges, teas, enemas, and cannulas, are all used, and promise to restore a "fresh and rosy color,"[4] "perfect health,"[5] a sentiment of the Ideal. Seen as tyrannical and deceptive, a symbol of bourgeois decorum and growing industrialization, this general purification is therefore caricatured and ridiculed, as much in the texts as in the illustrations of the "little" marginal press of the avant-garde,[6] particularly *Le Chat Noir*. It is not then by chance that the paper devotes a whole page to an ad for the purgative Géraudel:[7] the motif of the purge is recurrent and blackens its pages. More than a fin-de-siècle reappropriation of the carnivalesque, notably marked by a reversal of hierarchies that favors the "productive lower body,"[8] this motif is used in a more surprising way by Georges Fragerolle to define the *fumiste* esthetic, as practiced by the artists of *Le Chat Noir*:[9]

"*Fumisme* is to wit as the operetta is to the opéra bouffe, the cartoon to the caricature, the prune to Hunyadi-Janos water […] What, in short, is more profoundly *fumiste* than the prune, which, while presenting itself under the most benevolent exterior, contains in its bowels unexpected rebellions?"[10]

Although the analogy between purgation and the creative act is a cliché, readily synthesized in the verb *faire*[11] [to make], it is digested and remodeled according to the *fumiste* esthetic. Resting on a fundamental ambiguity, a method of writing that does not believe in itself, *fumisme* consists of a systematic distancing, of an always indirect statement, and even "reflected once, twice, often ten times," adds Georges Fragerolle. If writing is "making," *fumisme* superimposes the meaning of deceiving, of exploiting,[12] by mystifying the mind of the reader, "who loses his balance and laughs."[13]

Since *fumisme* supposes deceptive "exteriors," we shall have to question this art of "making" well, whether in a chamber pot or on a sheet of paper, in the sense of a general mystification, against the background of the fin-de-siècle crisis of the ideal and of artistic creation. Beyond its entertaining aspect, the motif of the purge, so necessary to the proper functioning of society, is overturned: by making the text malfunction, it reflects the *fumiste* process of creation.

Internal Dysfunctions

The motif of the purge is not only a fin-de-siècle avatar of the traditional evacuation and projection of excrement. Indeed, if the carnivalesque strives to overturn order, *fumisme*, organized "in complicity and exaggeration,"[14] puts everything in disorder. This cliché thus overflows its usual setting: it is not so much the act of defecation that interests the artists of *Le Chat Noir*, but the disturbance that precedes it. It is on this excess that the *fumiste* laugh is based: the characters are either stricken with diarrhea, or with the impossibility or inability to "make"; the thought of either one torments them and leads them from common logic, drives them mad. In "Faux toupet"[15] [False Nerve] by Alphonse Allais, Hercule, a young man, in love with his neighbor whose apartment is next to the bathroom on his floor, gets the idea to swallow "a bottle of Sedlitz water of uncommon strength," in the secret hope of meeting her. But although this voluntary purge gives him courage and, by means of chance meetings and languorous looks, allows him to seduce the young woman, in spite of everything he "loses it," in the true sense of the term: "Hercule had purged himself too much."[16] "Making" opens a hole, the one in Hercule's body, as well as a space that the lovers will never cross: sex has become impossible. This story seems above all a pretext for the exemplification of the binomial *colique* / *mélancolique*, a cliché the artists never tire of at *Le Chat Noir*,[17] to play on Hugo's definition of the pun, that "dropping of the mind," by taking it literally, wringing the neck of "spleen" in the process.

If too much purging derails the action, constipation blocks it. So, in the comedy by Henry Somm, *La Berline de l'Émigré ou jamais trop tard pour bien faire*[18] [*The Expatriate's Berlin, or Never Too Late to Make Good*], the chronic constipation of Madame Gardetout [from *garde tout*, "keeps everything"], a toilet attendant, is made the unusual pretext for her refusal to give Cantoisel the hand of her daughter, Léocadie. For, although he is one of their best customers,[19] her ideal son-in-law would be a "constipated man."[20] It is only thanks to a prank orchestrated by Waldemar de la Saladière, the expatriate with the berlin and the providential man who becomes Cantoisel's adoptive father, that Madame Gardetout's intestines will unblock and therefore allow the play to resolve on a happy ending: he takes advantage of the woman fainting to pour in her mouth a little "marvelous powder," brought back from one of his trips; the effect is immediate. Because of this prank, disguises are exchanged, the categories—here "him who make caca"[21] and he who cannot—crumble, leading to a "general indistinctness"[22] that is strictly *fumiste*.

Putting into disorder intestines as well as social categories extends to the unseemly confusion between *ordure* [excrement] and *or* [gold], a fault already present in society, because purgative sellers, toilet attendants, and septic tank cleaners earn their living this way. The artists of *Le Chat Noir* deflect it toward the absurd, by their hyperbolic treatment. In a wordless picture story by Doës,[23] the abusive aspect of this practice has as its corollary the intrusive insistence of the septic tank cleaner, who, in order to collect his fee, does not hesitate to surprise his client by coming through the hole of the toilet that the latter is preparing to fill. Paying for defecation gives rise to a paradox, for the shitter is doubly cleaned: "En échang' de votr' numéraire / On n'vous donne rien… au contraire!"[24] [In exchange for your cash / We give you nothing… On the contrary!] And its contrary is also true:

J'm'en allais, heureux comme un roi,
Quand la buralist' me rappelle:
—Votr' sou ne pass' plus!—me dit-elle!…
—Ah! lui dis-j', veuillez m'pardonner,
J'n'en ai pas d'autre à vous donner:
Il faut c'pendant qu'personn' n'y perde!…
Alors, ell' me répondit:… Zut!
Pour moi, je n'vois qu'un seul moyen:
C'est de r'prendr' tout bonnement votr' bien![25]

[I was leaving, as happy as a king,
When the tobacconist called me back:

"Your sou is stuck!" she tells me!…
"Ah," I say to her, "please excuse me,
I don't have another one to give you:
But no one must lose anything!…"
So, she answered: "…Damn!
For me, I can see only one way:
That's simply to take back your property!"]

In turn excreted, retaken, stolen, replaced, happening at the wrong time, as well as in the wrong place,[26] or not happening at all—thus the artists of *Le Chat Noir* amuse themselves by making shit appear and disappear, the better to confuse matters. But the motif of the purge is for them above all a way to depict concretely the deceptive tricks of *fumisme* that move from the thematic level to the level of statement. In fact, it is the deception itself that is staged. For example, in "Intempesive Substitution"[27] [Inopportune Substitution] by Doës, we find the expression *poser un lapin* [literally "to place a rabbit," figuratively "to stand someone up"]: a butcher replaces a soldier's diarrhea with the viscera of a rabbit; the soldier thinks he's emptied out his guts and dies of fright.

While the excremental material establishes itself as a mark of the negative, of failure, a failed laugh develops, which falls flat. Laughing at everything, but, by the "reflex" nature of this laugh, especially at himself, the *fumiste* artist radicalizes the deception: he constructs a way of writing that does not believe in itself, by a systematic distancing. The commonplace of the purge as a reflection of the creative act is thus reinvested to highlight the dysfunctions of fin-de-siècle creation.

Making Verses

"Making verses" usually tends to be insulting in *Le Chat Noir*.[28] Although the position of these artists on the process of creation is ambiguous—they take all its attempts the wrong way, both sophisticated theorizations and trivializations—they especially attack those they see as the real swindlers, the cheap poets, from the writer of doggerel to the "have-you-read-me,"[29] concerned only with selling his book. In fact, they set against them the fantastical vision of writing on an assembly line in a "factory,"[30] or its literal variation, intestinal worms [*vers* meaning both "verses" and "worms"] and other parasites:

Puis, faire des vers, trésor!—d'amour, de lard, ou d'ire,
Ou d'art.—Marrons sculptés au cycle où tu soupas.
[…]

Depuis cinq ou six grogs, je me prends aux cheveux
Pour accoucher enfin le poème nerveux
D'un jeune virulent qui m'a passé sa teigne.[31]

[Then, make verses, darling!—of love, of lard, or of anger,
Or of art.—Brown ones sculpted during the cycle when you dined.
[…]

For five or six grogs, I've been tearing my hair
To give birth at last to the vigorous poem
Of a virulent youth who gave me his ringworm.]

Anyone believes he can write, yet the secret is far from obvious. Exasperated by incessant questions from "idiots as curious as they are rudely ridiculous,"[32] Pimpinelli,[33] in "Révélation du Grand Turc ou l'art poétique mis à la portée de tous quelconques"[34] [Revelation of the Grand Turk, or the poetic art brought within the reach of everyone whatsoever], mockingly takes up the cliché of the prescribed enema:

Vous me demandez: «*Comment
L'on fais des vers?*» […]
[…]
Si rien ne vient, lors il urge
Qu'indécemment l'on vous purge.

You ask me: "*How
Does one make verses?*" […]
[…]
[If nothing comes, then it is urgent
That indecently you be purged.]

For it is indeed the "indecency" of such a request that requires a scatological poetic art. And for René Stalin to make light of it in "Histoire triste"[35] [Sad Story]: a young aspiring poet learns from his friend Harry Cower [that is, *haricot vert*, "green bean"] that Tobine, a successful poet, "would rhyme on command, especially on leaving the table, where for him, curious thing, ideas formed favorably";[36] having the occasion to picnic next to the poet, the young man discreetly follows him after the meal to learn his secret, which in the end is not revealed: Tobine is not necessarily a hoaxer, he simply suffers from diarrhea. The sphincter is thus made into a *fumiste* variation on the sphinx, the deceptive carrier of a message more vague than obscure. Although the secret of creation is preserved, the scene nevertheless inspires the perplexed narrator to "vers méla-n-coliques."[37] The pseudo-polyptoton depicts the breaking down of thought weakening into formlessness, like the deterioration of the rich rhyme ending in its anagrammatic reversal:

> Je réfléchis,
> Je fléchis,
> Je ch…
>
> [I reflect,
> I bend,
> I sh…]

The cliché of poetic art imitating a purge of the poet is here reversed into an art of shitting, a set of directions no doubt useful "to everyone whatsoever," even if the inconveniences of such a practice are not to be dismissed:

"Alphonse Allais, the distinguished chemist, just had a very interesting volume published by Germer-Baillière[38]: *On the influence of oil-based printing ink on hemorrhoids.*"[39]

To distort this commonplace is also a way for the poets of *Le Chat Noir* to critique the inspiration and methods of their Decadent colleagues. It is in fact easy for them to draw the connection between the motifs of decay and purgation. Jean des Deubourneau in "Mélancolie"[40] points out the banality of both of them, in an exultation parodistically disillusioned with listing the modalities of the obscene:

> Puisque nul n'aime ce ragout:
> L'Idéal fade, et que tout change,
> Si la vogue est à la Vidange,
> Poussons notre barque à l'égout.
>
> Fleurons les relents de cloaque,
> Les chiens crevés flottants et ronds;
> Soyons fins ciseleurs d'étrons;
> Mirons l'étoile dans la flaque.

Foin des tableaux jadis plaisants,
Chantons le pus et les névroses,
Crachons au cœur vermeil des roses,
Et pissons sur les vers luisants!

[Since nobody likes this stew,
The drab Ideal, and everything changes,
If the fashion is for Drainage,
Let us push our boat to the sewer.

Let us stink of the stench of the cesspool,
Of floating and bloated dead dogs;
Let us be fine chiselers of turds;
Let us mirror the star in the puddle.

To hell with the old pleasant pictures,
Let us sing of pus and neuroses,
Let us spit on the scarlet heart of roses,
And piss on glow-worms / shining verses!]

But, although the poets of *Le Chat Noir* mock those "fine chiselers of turds," and do not chisel golden or "shining verses" themselves, they still produce depictions of purgation from the points of their pens. Let us repeat the verses already cited:

Je réflechis,
Je fléchis,
Je ch…

The suspension points are not added from consideration for the reader, or to stymie censorship, but contribute to a visual suggestion of the basely productive act:

. . . .
La ceinture ardente du rêve
Sangle mon désir déchainé…
—Je sens le ballon qui s'enlève,
Et je n'ai pas encore dîné.[41]

118

[. . . . .
The burning belt of the dream
Cinches my unleashed desire…
—I feel the ball come out,
And I have not yet dined.]

This punctuation neither suspends nor completes the poem; its scope extends beyond, or beneath, the poetic statement, like the carnivalesque body that is open and in perpetual expansion, and the *fumiste* laughter continues through it. Assuming the role of "ink shitters,"[42] and like those shitters who cover latrine walls with "commas,"[43] the poets of *Le Chat Noir* reinvest this "excremental punctuation"[44] by making it the mark of the *fumiste* subversion of writing. Thus, the "reflex" movement of the deceptive "prune" takes on the appearance of a *bifur*,[45] between an unexpected bifurcation and a distorting deletion, as shown for example in Verlaine's "Pantoum négligé"[46] [Slovenly Pantoum]: "three little blots, a period and comma." Although Verlaine claims here to practice an impromptu writing, taken from life, malleable according to his imagination, he lays out a series of signs without unity, ink stains swollen and then wiped from the surface of the page, mimicking both the slips of purgation and those of the quest for poetic perfection. "Making" "twice, often ten times,"[47] rather than perfecting. Excess is converted into emptiness, and inversely. Thus the "colossal Voice of shadow" in "Symphonie en noir majeur"[48] [Symphony in black major] by Geo. Bonneron expresses itself with this "excremental punctuation" and "says"[49] nothing:

Alors la Voix parla, colossale Voix d'ombre,
Plus lente que la Nuit, plus profonde et plus sombre…
Elle dit: . . . .

[Then the Voice spoke, colossal Voice of shadow,
Slower than the Night, deeper and darker…
It said: . . . .]

The contradictory use of this punctuation seems to depict a "border zone"[50] of the lyric afflatus.

A Diarrheal Lyric Afflatus?

For if there is one thing that malfunctions in this fin-de-siècle period, it is certainly lyricism. Subverting its codes is a prerequisite for the avant-garde, notably by shifting the lyric afflatus to make it blow from the anus:[51] "petomania" is then in fashion. Only what is specific to *Le Chat Noir* is that this release of air vacillates between inflation and deflation, like the pump of Maurice Mac-Nab's subject-irrigator.[52] It thus occurs in a movement that is doubled, contradictory, unstable, between overturned demiurgic power and hazy confusion, containing as much opaque matter as emptiness. Therefore, "Désillusion"[53] by Charles Poisson shows the play not of optical illusions, but of sonic disillusionment:

"An inexpressible anguish invaded the poet. He sought the sacred word that could express his blissful admiration, the words that could paint his delight [...]. Then he grew bolder: 'O you,' he said, 'before whom I prostrate myself with latria, under whose steps flowers germinate, corollas blossom, ravish my clouded soul with the sound of your sweet voice, ineffable symphony of lyre or Aeolian harp.'

"He waited, anxious. His right hand, which embraced her waist, lowered shamelessly, assuring itself of the materiality of her hips, when a noise arose under his hand, at the bottom of the vocal cords: a sound at first as soft as an unobtrusive breath, then trumpeting, a flatulence leaving in the atmosphere a vague mephitic stench.

"Then, his dream stillborn, he fled in shame, reflecting on how sad the sound of the body is under the fingers."

In effect, *fumisme* acts like a sounding board,[54] a sonic variation on smoke and mirrors, and because of this is more impalpable, vague, evanescent. Alfred de Vigny's famous line, "God! How sad the sound of the horn is deep in the woods!"[55] is here diffracted[56] and rendered absurd, with puns on *corps* and *cor* ("body" and "horn") and *doigts* and *bois* ("fingers" and "woods"): all these sounds, the empty words of the smooth-talking poet, the young woman's "Aeolian" response, the stupid joke of the final parody, overlap, echo one another, forming a diarrheal hubbub, a joke within a joke within a joke. An exercise as futile and inconsistent as it is effective, in its studied simultaneity, which endlessly deceives, makes mistakes itself, in order to "make" better, to "make [...] at all costs."[57] Making the air into a new space, better for speech to fall flat, where one can truly "experiment with limits."[58] In *Le Chat Noir*, the cliché of the purge takes all its meaning in the void that it creates. Just as the purge opens bellies, *fumisme* opens the gaps in the text, leaving to poetic creation the space to talk to oneself, or not to talk to oneself, and to the *fumiste* avatar of the grain of salt, the "prune," to infiltrate the workings of the lyric afflatus.

In fact, "making" well seems to signal to the persistence of a possible lyricism, as twisting as the intestines, which will function in spite of everything. The axis is no longer the vertical one, sustained by traditional lyricism, nor the preservation of an alternative elevation, promulgated by the intestines (as in "Anatomie"[59] by Eugène Godin: "*The intestines*—I arise"), but another way, reflexive, resonant. The goal is a performative speech that would play out "in the obscure labyrinth of muscular tissues, / In muted stomach grumbling."[60] What is important is that the "Flatuosité: Musique de Foire"[61] [Flatulence: Music for the Fair / Diarrhea] make itself heard, play us its little tune on the pipe, here[62] and now.

The *fumiste* "prune" distorts the structure of the texts or illustrations, corrupts their composition, gives them diarrhea. Deceptive turd or careless chiseling, it opens a zone of indeterminacy that it destabilizes and blurs: the cliché of the purge joins the performativity inherent in lyricism, satisfies the quest for the immediate reaction of the collective laughter experienced at *Le Chat Noir*, all playing out in a "reflex" movement within the interstices of speech. Assuredly, although all this arises from a contiguous story of viscera and derrières, it is important to resist "derriérisme,"[63] to distance oneself, to "make" one's own hole.

CHAPTER TEN

On the Little Illnesses That We Enjoy

Le Ver Solitaire

Aussi je m'en vais par la route
Faire des vers… très bien, sans doute!
Des vers à tort et à travers,
Mais des vers quand même, des vers![1]

[Furthermore I go off on the road
To make verses… very well, no doubt!
Verses willy-nilly,
But verses all the same, verses!]

Georges Lorin

Whereas ever since Baudelaire, literature has done its utmost to show illness, preferably incurable and therefore leading to a lingering death, depicting it as horribly as possible—the ambient decay is incarnated in deformed, oozing, ulcerated bodies, rotting on their feet—the artists in the "little" fin-de-siècle papers, in keeping with their status, prefer minor diseases, temporary ailments, like the corns sung by Maurice Mac-Nab,[2] and moving on to diarrhea,[3] passing through a case of rheumatism that actually is not.[4] Le Chat Noir, proceeding by both "childish and coarse simplification"[5] and an updating of medical knowledge—the scientific avant-garde in the person of Pasteur, in particular—is interested in little invisible illnesses, to the extent that they result from micro-organisms or evolve inside the body.[6] This zoom effect has as its corollary a readjustment of the language: it is not so much the symptoms the writers enjoy listing as the microbes themselves. If Decadent language is so fixated on pathologies that it becomes one itself, the artists of Le Chat Noir emphasize their visceral refusal of pathos: it is a matter of tasting these new words, reveling in them, enjoying them in another way, namely literally. So, in those times of "acute literaturitis,"[7] of making "verses indiscriminately,"[8] it is not by chance that, in the organ of the press that interests us, the most symptomatic disease is tapeworm, which it is therefore fitting to investigate in a group setting. Although it complements—among other diseases—the dishes at first, we shall also see that, having become a character in its own right, it has troubles of its own, in the sense that it is made to suffer a certain number of misadventures. Under the cover of provocation, even bad taste, the issue for these artists is simultaneously subverting and dramatizing the famous fin-de-siècle "crisis of verse"[9] (*vers* meaning, always, both "verses" and "worms").

A Feast of Diseases

The link from cause to effect can seem elliptical as well as absurd in these verses by Camille de Sainte-Croix, particularly the last line:

Une fortune—un déshonneur.
Un baiser—une jalousie.
Une ripaille—une phtisie.[10]

[A fortune—a dishonor.
A kiss—a jealousy.
A feast—a phthisis.]

The suggested phenomenon, however, is proven scientifically by fin-de-siècle discoveries and the advent of microbiology: microbes are found not only in waste or rotting matter, but everywhere, including in food still considered fit for consumption. Simply by feeding himself, every individual thus has to ingest thousands of microbes and bacteria, of all kinds, and is consequently susceptible to falling ill. Except that in *Le Chat Noir*, this most banal of procedures assumes exaggerated proportions. The smallest dish is transformed into a veritable profusion of pathologies and contagious diseases.

The codes of the feast are reworked and pushed to their extreme. All the varieties of microbes are enumerated. Raoul Ponchon, known for the bacchic and culinary vein in his songs, does not neglect adding them to his repertory. He therefore compiles a non-exhaustive list of the microscopic worms nestled in a salad:

Échinocoque, trichocéphale-dispar,
Anguillule, amœba coli, lombricoïdale
Ascarides, ankylostome nicobar,
Oxyure vermiculaire, balantide…
J'en passe et des meilleurs. Tels sont, mes chers enfants,
Entre mille autres, qui vivent à nos dépens,

Les vers intestinaux. […]
Quand nous faisons intervenir, dans nos festins,
Ce que vous appelez, moi de même, salade.[11]

[Echinococcus, Trichocephalus dispar,
Eelworm, Entamoeba coli, Ascaris
Lumbricoides, Ancylostoma nicobarica,
Oxyuris vermicularus, balantidium…
To only name a few. These are, my dear children,
Among a thousand others, which live at our expense,
The intestinal worms. […]
When we bring in, at our feasts,
What you call, as do I, salad.]

Feeding oneself on diseases is not just a fin-de-siècle avatar of the carnivalesque banquet.[12] Whereas the carnivalesque strives to overturn order, the *chatnoiresque* esthetic puts everything in disorder. The use of words becomes vague, and with them their meanings, so that however we might say or see it, the writers show that we are always dealing with garbage: we "eat a pile of filth that shameless restauranteurs call mutton stew or beef croquettes: within them swarms a world of microscopic worms that scientists call microbes."[13]

This linguistic disorder extends to social behavior. The feast in question is the product of society, in every sense of the word: minor diseases are both caused by humans and commercialized by them. Despite the apparent incongruity of such production, the artists of *Le Chat Noir* combine these two modalities to assert one of the paradoxes of life: it proceeds from a massive recycling of little ailments, not to mention little deaths, in food. Gaston Dumestre thus recalls that in Paris, the daily water comes from the Seine and that, in this same river, float "stiffs," the privileged living place of "maggots":

Sur leur abdomen, les vers blancs
Se marient et font des enfants
Imitant de leurs père et mère
Le couple amoureux et prospère;
La tribu dans ce sentiment
S'accroit considérablement.

Leur odorante pourriture

Est le meilleur champ de culture
Du choléra car dans Paris,
Par chacun ce liquide est pris
Et tout habitant doit en boire,
C'est gratuit et obligatoire.[14]

[On their abdomen, the maggots
Marry and have children
Imitating the prosperous and loving couples
Of their fathers and mothers;
With those feelings, the tribe
Grows considerably.

Their fragrant putrefaction
Is the best field for growing
Cholera, for in Paris,
This liquid is taken by everyone,
And every inhabitant must drink it,
It's free and obligatory.]

As for J. Derriaz, he reiterates the point that the shit produced by the vernal activity of purgation serves to fertilize the earth for "future victuals,"[15] some of which will be used for new purges:

Et tout le genre humain procède
À son curage intestinal.

Ainsi, de ses propres entrailles,
Tirant les sucs réconfortants
Dont se nourrissent les semailles,
À ses propres victuailles
L'homme pourvoit chaque printemps.

[…]
Son impur résidu se change
En bons plats d'épinards qu'on mange
Pour se purifier le sang.
. . . .

[And the whole human race carries out

126

Its intestinal cleaning.

So, from his own entrails,
Drawing the comforting juices
That nourish the crops,
Every spring man provides
For his own entrails.

[...]
His impure residue changes into
Good plates of spinach, which are eaten
To purify the blood.
. . . .]

This cynical vision of the reality of the body favors the shift toward a representation of society that combines black humor, strangeness, and science fiction. The recycling of minor ailments is readapted to growing industrialization and the laws of the marketplace, and in this way pushed to its height. Diseases are presented as a virtually perfect first matter. In an economic column,[16] Xernand Fau cannot praise them enough. They are "unlimited resources," and access to them is facilitated by the intermediary of hospitals, which are "an inexhaustible source": diseases are, besides, "natural products," not to mention free for the taking. Fau gives several examples of reconditioning: tapeworms "provide appetizing noodles, which will free us from the enormous price we pay Italy"; "at the Children's Hospital, every death will as an immediate corollary be prepared either with blanquette or Marengo"; diabetics would give their sugar for the use of all refineries. This idea of making the recycling of diabetes into a business is taken up a few years later by Maurice Curnonsky. What begins as an unpublished interview with Cornélius Herz, the exiled businessman implicated in the Panama scandal (1892), veers off into a gastronomical tale.[17] While the journalist tries to grill Herz on this thorny affair, the latter offers him a dinner whose peculiarity is that all of the dishes are sweet: "Lobster in brown sugar sauce / Chaud-froid of duck and sugarcane / Presweetened leg of lamb" etc. Curnonsky elaborates on the two troubles plaguing the real Herz, the diabetes mellitus that prevents him from attending his trial and his greed for money. Herz—the one in the story—turns this "providential diabetes"[18] into a lucrative food-processing business. Daily harvests from his own body allow him to produce a sugar with novel properties, for the pure and soluble extract of diabetes possesses "prodigious saccharifying power: 2 centigrams is enough to sweeten a bowl containing ten pounds of cherries." Illnesses, even when not contagious, are passed on to others. Besides, Curnonsky does not fail to develop the metaphor. Herz ends by offering several grams of this "prodigious" powder to the journalist who came to interview him, who himself suggests that the readers of *Le Chat Noir* can win it as a gift.

The feast of diseases is thus not only a satire on scientific interest in the microscopic, it is a question of mocking a self-sufficient society, with customs that are as grotesque, even obscene, as they are contradictory. When we peer into the microscope, the zoom effect imposes itself, even if it borders on the excessive. It is also a depiction of the *chatnoiresque* art, since from a mere nothing—a microbe—the writers turn the text toward the incredible, so that what is usually eaten appears inedible, and the worms that are expelled are themselves swallowed. Poetic justice in such a context: let the diseases have a taste!

The Trials and Tribulations of the Tapeworm

The totem animal of the paper is, of course, the black cat. This animal, a symbol of freedom, is the hero of numerous stories, drawings, and poems. It defines the identity of the group, just as it represents its cohesion. But another "animalcule"[19] seems also to have some importance. And if the tapeworm as a hero is incontestably an additional provocation, the *chatnoiresque* logic ups the ante by playing on the confusion between the homophones: the two are equal. If the worm is tortured, parasitized, killed, it is because it metaphorizes verse, in particular the kind then in fashion, free verse. In the mocking eyes of *Le Chat Noir*, it can only free itself.

Tapeworms are most often humanized. Each has a name, even a last name; some educate themselves, especially by reading; one plays cards;[20] another drinks until it's as "drunk as thirteen Polish tapeworms."[21] However, the *chatnoiresque* tapeworm has the specificity of never being alone.[22] By its very nature, the other is established as a systematic element of disturbance, and consequently is the cause of all its woes and even its death. For example, a story by Gaston Dumestre[23] tells how the peaceful life of Glab-Réfèbe (that is, *glabre éphèbe*, "hairless ephebe") comes to a sudden end: because of "a dirty trick," he finds himself forced to share his den with another worm, Faune-Étique ("boneless animal,": but also *phonétique*). The latter, "fateful premonition, looked like a long BLACK ribbon, which had been bleached." In order to preserve their status as "solitary worm," they decide to fight a duel, according to the following terms: they will race from the rectum to the esophagus, and the first to arrive will eat the other. But the affair turns into tragedy: "The race of the two tapeworms had caused so much commotion in the Man's belly that he died and… stopped eating, as is common in this circumstance." And the "winning" tapeworm, obviously, starves to death. The refusal of the other, the fact that he is imprisoned, that he is antisocial—he shows himself just as scornful of his host as of his fellows—or even misogynistic, are so many characteristics that the tapeworm shares with that social type so topical at the fin de siècle, the bachelor.[24] Besides, inversely, didn't the Goncourt brothers call the latter a "parasite at the social banquet"?[25] The bachelor upsets the bourgeois order because he refuses to reproduce himself, and would place, in fact, "the nation in danger."[26] Society therefore judges him useless at his proper function. "The tapeworm is always a bachelor,"[27] we read in the columns of Le Chat Noir; this does not stop Gaston Dumestre from inventing a son for Glabre-Éphèbe (as he was then spelled), in a sequel to the story,[28] a son who is married and bitterly regrets it. He compares his wife to "a monster, a python, a hydra, the Hydra of Lerna," at whose "heels he will drag all his life." Although the idea of a tapeworm ironically parasitized by another until death ensues is repeated, the sequel is above all an opportunity for the writer to include a pun on the *Hydropathes*, the precursors of Le Chat Noir. The poor tapeworm in fact finds himself saddled with the nickname "Glabre-Éphèbe-hydre-aux-pattes tout court" [just Hairless-Ephebe-hydra-with-legs], with a pun on *hydre-aux-pattes* and *Hydropathes*.

This reference emphasizes a metapoetic reactualization of the motif of the "solitary worm" at the level of Le Chat Noir. The agony of the worm never ceases to reenact mockingly that of academic verse, in short the crisis that assails it and which is exacerbated by the "little" papers. It is not for nothing that they could be compared to "hothouses"[29] where one might "grow the seeds"[30] of certain poetic innovations or mutations. This is particularly the case with free verse. Not only does it become fashionable in avant-garde movements, but furthermore a fierce battle is waged between them for the right to its paternity. The polemic intensifies among critics of all perspectives—Charles Maurras, Georges Rodenbach, Rachilde, among others!; it also divides the poets among them, such as Jules Laforgue, Gustave Kahn, and Marie Krysinska.[31] The inclusion of this last, who participated in the *Hydropathes* and contributed to Le Chat Noir, involves to some extent the paper that interests us in this affair. However, in keeping with the *fumiste* spirit that they proclaim, the editors of Le Chat Noir maintain an ambiguous position toward the question of free verse. The situation is not lacking in spice; it is a question of laughing at it and using it as the pretext for various scenarios. If it is called "free," it is because the worm/verse is capable of freeing itself, in other words escaping the body of its host. Such a case occurs in the parodistic collection by Gabriel Vicaire and Henri Beauclair, the famous *Déliquescences d'Adoré Floupette* (1885):

> Les Tænias
> Que tu nias
> Traîtreusement s'en sont allés.[32]

> [The Tapeworms
> That you denied
> Have treacherously gone away.]

Although older, the text of Charles Leroy, "Skating-bière ou l'Asticot de la Providence"[33] [Skating-bier or the Maggot of Providence], provides a premonitory vision. A tapeworm tries in fact to escape the corpse of its late landlord, but the undertakers, in a hurry to finish the funeral, do not agree; especially because the tapeworm, one of whose rings is caught, flees with the coffin:

"Frightened, he decided to flee. […] he started to pull both the coffin and his ex-landlord […] The undertakers […] try to seize the maggot by the neck, but in vain: he runs, he flies, and the coffin follows like an arrow."

The length of this kind of verse is constantly mocked. Although Georges Camuset establishes a (relative) similarity between the feet in his sonnet "Le Ver solitaire" [The Solitary Worm] and those of the worm—"One must respect / The profound feeling that moves me to sing / In verses of twelve feet the worm of twelve meters."[34]—the use of free verse distorts this bit of data. The worm/verse is referred to as sick: it is said to suffer from a "sickness of length."[35] It is "sometimes thirty feet long,"[36] and up to "ninety-six feet,"[37] as the "I" poet boasts in "Chanson bancale" [Lopsided Song]:

> Et j'ai surpris tout l'or du soir sur une cuvelle
> Et je tourne la manivelle.
> —Lorsque mes vers ont quatre-vingt-seize pieds,
> On ne peut pas émettre cette idée que c'est l'ampleur qui leur manque.

> [And I surprised all the evening gold on a tub
> And I turn the crank.

—When my verses have ninety-six feet,
Nobody can express that idea that it is magnitude that they lack.]

However, the "profound analogy between the organic and the poetic"[38] of these respective worms/lines is not confined to the sole problem of length. Alfred Béjot thus offers a (false) analysis that is more advanced:

"It appears that such worms (called 'solitary' because they do not rhyme (3)) are ordinarily not excreted except by the aid of some drug (haschisch or pumpkin seed). […]

"(3) One will note other similarities between Symbolist verse and the tapeworm, namely that it is flat, that it is sometimes thirty feet long, and that it usually divides into slices of unequal sizes."[39]

On the model of a language that is dissolving, the solitary worm/verse leaves the expected framework of prosodic rules, but is not limited to that. "The verse proliferates"[40] and gradually contaminates all forms of writing.

Solitary Worms / Verses in the Group Setting

Marc Angenot notes that such an abundance of verse in the 1890s overflows the strictly poetic genre: "In these times of universal 'poetry,' even the journalist expresses himself in verse."[41] Although the position of the *Chat Noir* artists on this phenomenon is ambiguous, they attack whatever seems to give them indigestion. Faced with the "microbe of poetry,"[42] the latest endemic pathology—the one before it had been love—they counter it with prose texts mimicking scientific discourse. They take the opposite view of attempts at both the banalization of poetry and sophisticated theorizations. On the one hand is the fantastical vision of scientists explaining the discovery of the microbe, this "monster,"[43] its isolation, the different experiments they perform, especially the inoculation of concierges, who write their rent receipts in verse.[44] On the other hand, it is an opportunity to critique the style and esthetic of Symbolist poetry, then as much in vogue as contagion. Charles Aubertin writes a mock report from the Academy of Medicine on the "use of Symbolist poems and the dangers it may present"[45] for the health of readers as well as for their journalistic colleagues. In fact, there would have been a diagnosis of "exaggerated intoxication" particularly among "critics and directors of young magazines," and even a certain number of "sudden deaths" due to the cerebral effort required when faced with the complexity and obscurity of these verses.

Making the "solitary worm" a recurrent motif is not then just a vulgar joke on the part of the *Chat Noir* artists, but constitutes precisely a reaction against the abundance of works in verse. And although its use can seem at first like a parodistic game, it contributes even more to a certain cohesion of the group.

In both the paper and cabaret, art is lived and practiced collectively. A very marked intertextuality links the texts to one another. This is for example the case with the parodies written of the famous "Sonnet d'Arvers"[46] [Sonnet by Arvers]. This elegiac sonnet evokes the suffering of a love that is unreciprocated and consequently leaves the "I" "solitary." A few verses, as a reminder:

Mon âme a son secret, ma vie a son mystère,
Un amour éternel en un moment conçu:
[…]
Hélas! j'aurai passé près d'elle inaperçu,
Toujours à ses côtés, et pourtant solitaire.

[My soul has its secret, my life has its mystery,
An eternal love conceived in one moment:
[…]
Alas! I would have passed close to her unnoticed,
Always at her side, and yet solitary.]

Parodying this often ridiculed sonnet is in no way profoundly *chatnoiresque*, it is even a common practice.[47] The next to last line ("the verses all filled with her" in the original version) particularly inspired erotic variations, including from Victor Hugo!: "Hélas! J'aurai piné près d'elle inaperçu, / Sans me l'asticoter et pourtant solitaire."[48] [Alas! I would have fucked close to her unnoticed, / Without having to deal with her, and yet solitary.] The presence of the verb *asticoter* ("to bother", from *asticot*, "maggot") brings us back to our story of the tapeworm. The specificity of the *chatnoiresque* treatment rests precisely on the use made of the term "solitary." For these artists, it systematically recalls the related worm. Jean Goudezki, in his "Sonnet de revers *ou l'angoisse d'un ministre déchu*"[49] [Sonnet of Setbacks, *or the anguish of a fallen minister*], thus writes:

Aussi rampant qu'un ver et non moins solitaire
Et je vais retourner à mes pommes de terre.

[As crawling as a worm and no less solitary
And I shall return to my potatoes.]

But the mechanism of variation deteriorates in *Le Chat Noir*, the "solitary worm" crawls toward other forms than a parody of Arvers. The interest lies in repeating the association of the lyric subject with the tapeworm, which quickly becomes a viral joke, but especially a ritual one. It must be emphasized that the only poem from the *Déliquescences d'Adoré Floupette* that the paper quotes in its entirety is precisely one about "Tænias" [Tapeworms]. In this way it joins the group game, establishing the attributive metaphor as a syntagm necessary for recognition among initiates:

Les Tænias
Que tu nias
Traitreusement s'en sont allés.

Dans la pénombre
Ma clameur sombre
A fait fleurir des azalées

Pendant les nuits
Mes longs ennuis
Brillent ainsi qu'un flambeau clair:

De cette perte
Mon âme est verte:
C'est moi qui suis le solitaire![50]

[The Tapeworms
That you denied
Have treacherously gone away.

In the twilight
My somber cry
Made azaleas bloom.

During the night
My long ennuis

Shine like a bright torch:

> From this loss
> My soul is peeved:
> It is I who am the solitary!]

A metaphor we find again in "Le Ver solitaire" by Vincent Hyspa, but in the form of a leitmotiv—a worm/verse that is often reappropriated: "I am the poor worm, the poor solitary worm."[51] So, this play on words is both a rallying symbol and a vector of recognition between colleagues within the group. It is, in fact, on singing this text for the first time at the *Chat Noir* cabaret,[52] with a serious and impassive air,[53] that Hyspa not only made himself noticed, but accepted as an equal. Maurice Donnay compares the event to a metamorphosis: "This piece about a worm flew up to the skies [*nues*], like a worm! [with a pun on *nu comme un ver*, naked as a worm]"[54] Hyspa becomes not a butterfly, but a Black Cat: "Ever since that evening, you were from Montmartre. At the same time, you became our childhood friend and schoolmate!"[55] Paradoxically, claiming this solitary (worm) condition is a way for the group to show its cohesion and specificity.

The dialogism does not, however, stop with the repetition of this one syntagm. The paper is in effect a forum, where the contributors write and respond to one another, especially in verse. We return to the feast of diseases: the reading of another contributor's verse is compared to tasting. This produces some drolly bizarre passages, if one takes into account the ricocheting play of echoes between words, things, and individuals. These excerpts from three poems, with different writers and addressees, testify to the inextricable tangle that this organic and tortuous motif never ceases to recreate among its various meanings:

> De ta jolie épître en vers
> Gloutonnement je me régale[56]

> Mes remerciements sincères
> Sont pour toi quand tu me dis
> Qu'avec plaisir tu m'insères
> Des vers tous les samedis.[57]

> À lire hebdomadairement
> Tes envois aux rimes câlines,
> J'éprouve plaisir de gourmand

Savourant d'exquises pralines;
Oui, tes vers ont un goût très fin,
Bien qu'un peu beaucoup éphémère,
Avec leur distique à la fin
(Amande douce ou bien amère!).[58]

[On your lovely letter in verse
Gluttonously I feast.

My sincere thanks
To you when you tell me
That with pleasure you insert
My verses/worms every Saturday.

On reading weekly
Your dispatches in caressing rhymes,
I experience the pleasure of a gourmand
Savoring exquisite pralines;
Yes, your verses have a very delicate taste,
Even though a bit too ephemeral,
With their couplet at the end
(Sweet or very bitter almond!)]

Playing cheerfully with the syllepsis[59] around the word *vers*, the artists of *Le Chat Noir* ridicule a poetic crisis that is already well established, but such a feast only ends up nauseating them. While academic verse seemed to be deteriorating in favor of less strict techniques, another invertebrate was hatching, free verse, which has nothing free about it except its name, since it becomes so parasitized itself by the Symbolists. According to the *Chat Noir* group, only those who escape being put in a box are free, whether it be an apothecary jar or theories that stifle their initial originality. And because the tapeworm figures among the (very) great (worms) forgotten by literature, it is all the more appreciated by *Le Chat Noir*, which no longer understands it as a disease, but as the antidote to that troubled period. In reaction to the tenacity of serious discourse, the group opts for an ardent imagination that "I don't know where it's taking us,"[60] if not into the "smallest room in the house" of literature.

❧ N O T E S ❧

NOTES

Introduction

[1] See especially Raymond de Casteras, *Avant le Chat Noir, Les Hydropathes*, Paris, Messein, 1945.

[2] He is the editor in chief until n° 111, 23 February 1884 (inclusive).

[3] Under this name, the artists cited above, or most of them, gather from 1881 to 1883, first around Maurice Petit, then around Émile Goudeau. Although the meetings at the Café de l'Avenir are regular and just as lively as those of the Hydropathes, the Hirsutes do not publish a periodical, which leads, perhaps, to their rapid decline.

[4] Raymond de Casteras, *op. cit.*, 30.

[5] Rodolphe Salis, "Notre Programme," *Le Chat Noir* [from now on, abbreviated in these notes to *CN*], Supplement to n° 1, 15 January 1882.

[6] Notably "La Ballade du Chat Noir chantée par Bonnet au Pavillon de l'Horloge" by Aristide Bruant, illustrated by Steinlen (*CN*, n° 135, 9 August 1884).

[7] Aristide Bruant installs his cabaret at the *Chat Noir's* former address, 84 boulevard Rochechouart.

[8] François Trombert is in fact originally from Lyon. In 1893, he founds the Cabaret des Quat'z'Arts, in Montmartre, then an eponymous paper in 1897, where one finds, as editor, Émile Goudeau.

[9] Louis Marsolleau, "Le Chat Noir," *CN*, n° 180, 20 June 1885.

[10] Such as *Phryné*, written by Maurice Donnay, first performed on 9 January 1891.

[11] For example "Le Violon vivant" (*CN*, n° 459, 1 November 1890).

[12] These columns appear weekly throughout 1882.

[13] Among others, "Histoire mirificque d'un moyne et d'une anguille qui n'estoit poinct de Melun" (*CN*, n° 180, 20 June 1885).

[14] We refer the reader to Daniel Grojnowski's work on this type of humor, especially *Aux Commencements du Rire moderne—L'Esprit fumiste* (Paris, José Corti, 1997), *Comiques d'Alphonse Allais à Charlot* (Villeneuve d'Ascq, Presses Universitaires du Septentrion, collection "Objet," 2004), and the anthology, in collaboration with Bernard Sarrazin, on *L'Esprit fumiste et les Rires fin de siècle* (Paris, José Corti, 1990).

[15] Georges Fragerolle, "Le Fumisme," *L'Hydropathe*, 2nd year, n° 8, 12 May 1880.

[16] This is the title he gives one of his collections of comic stories, published by Paul Ollendorff in 1891.

[17] Georges Japy, "Chronique parisienne," *La Vie moderne*, n° 7, 12 February 1887, 100-101.

[18] *Id.*

[19] Jean de La Fontaine, "Le Loup, la Chèvre et le Chevreau," *Fables*, Paris, Nepveu et L. de Bure, 1826, 184-185.

[20] Bernard Sarrazin, "Présentation II," in *L'Esprit fumiste et les rires fin de siècle*, ed. cit., 35.

[21] Émile Goudeau, *Dix ans de bohème* [1888], followed by *Les Hirsutes* by Léo Trézénik, Presentation by Michel Golfier and Jean-Didier Wagneur, with the collaboration of Patrick Ramseyer, Paris, Champ Vallon, 2000, 149.

[22] *Ibid.*, 151.

PART ONE: A POLYPHONIC GROUPISM

CHAPTER ONE:
Group Logic

[1] Each participant is portrayed in turn on the cover.

[2] Charles Cros, "Vertige," *CN*, n° 123, 17 May 1884.

[3] *CN*, n° 77, 30 June 1883.

[4] *Id*. Let us also quote Léon Durocher, "Montmartre!", *CN*, n° 418, 18 January 1890: "Butte sainte, à tes quatre vents / […] nous mêlons notre chanson / Et […] vibrent à l'unisson / Nos âmes… / Nous sommes les gais Montmartrois, / Gais d'être gueux, gais d'être rois / Du vague pays de Bohème, / Fiers de narguer le sens commun." [Holy hill, to your four winds / […] we mix our song / And […] vibrate in unison / Our souls… / We are the gay Montmartrois / Gay to be beggars, gay to be kings / Of the vague country of Bohemia, / Proud to defy common sense.]

[5] X., "Ballade des Assassins," *CN*, n° 19, 20 May 1882.

[6] *CN*, n° 614, 28 October 1893.

[7] Pierre Bourdieu, *Les Règles de l'art—Genèse et structure du champ littéraire*, Paris, éditions du Seuil, "Points Essais," 1992, 234.

[8] Maurice Donnay, *Mes Débuts à Paris*, Paris, Fayard, 1937, 278.

[9] *CN,* n° 121, 3 May 1884.

[10] *CN*, n° 1, 14 January 1882.

[11] Vox Populi, *CN*, n° 56, 3 February 1883.

[12] Alphonse Allais, *CN*, n° 22, 10 June 1882.

[13] Matou, *CN*, n° 28, 22 July 1882.

[14] See especially *CN*, n° 3, 28 January 1882 and *CN*, n° 9, 11 March 1882.

[15] Jules Jouy, "Les Pensées du Chat Noir" *CN*, n° 63, 24 March 1883.

[16] We are thinking here particularly of Pindar's Pythian Ode IV.

[17] Jacques Lehardy [Clément Privé], "Montmartre," *CN*, n° 1, 14 January 1882.

[18] *Id.*

[19] Louis Marsolleau, "Le Chat Noir," *CN*, n° 180, 20 June 1885.

[20] Daniel Grojnowski, "Présentation," in *L'Esprit fumiste et les rires fin de siècle*, ed. cit., 10.

[21] Fanciful dedicatory epigraphs to the wordless picture stories designate Sarcey as "irremovable uncle of *Le Chat Noir*." (Fernand Fau, "Place de la Concorde," *CN*, n° 367, 26 January 1889), and "our vertiginous, titanic, and forty times unique uncle Francisque Sarcey" (Doës, "Les jolis pieds du lieutenant Trippmann," *CN*, n° 364, 5 January 1889). He is not however their only "uncle": the status of "our new uncle" is for example granted to Ernest Legrouvé fils (among others, in Doës, "La Collation interrompue," *CN*, n° 327, 14 April 1888) and H. de Lapommeraye (Gorguet, "Avant le bal," *CN*, n° 331, 19 May 1888).

[22] One is reminded of the pseudonym Raymondo de la Cazba: *casbah* is slang for "house." This pseudonym seems to have been borrowed by Raymond d'Abzac.

[23] Paul Verlaine, *Poèmes saturniens*, Paris, Lemerre, 1866. The letter is dated 22 April 1867 (Victor Hugo, *Œuvres Complètes*, t. XIII, Paris, Le Club français du livre, 1972, 789).

[24] Edmond Lepelletier, *Paul Verlaine, Sa Vie—Son Œuvre*, Paris, Le Mercure de France, 1907, 141.

[25] Adolphe Willette, "Nana et Sahib—Conte hindou pour amuser Colibri," *CN*, n° 104, 5 January 1884.

[26] Aristide Bruant, "La Ballade du Chat Noir," *CN*, n° 135, 9 August 1884.

[27] We can cite the *fumiste* monologues of Charles Cros.

[28] For example, "La Ballade du Chat Noir," by Aristide Bruant, illustrated by Steinlen (*CN*, n° 135, 9 August 1884).

[29] In connection to the poem "P. P. C." by Émile Goudeau, one can also see a score by Léo Montancey and an illustration by Willette (*CN*, n° 67, 21 April 1883).

[30] Such as "Pierrot Bec-Salé" by Willette, which is given an "explanation" by A'Kempis [Émile Goudeau] (*CN*, n° 21, 3 June 1882).

[31] Accessible at the Bibliothèque Historique de la Ville de Paris, Ms. Res. 140, 88.

[32] This is for example the case with "La Dompteuse" by Fernand Crésy and "Le Dompteur" by Jules de Marthold (*CN*, n° 18, 13 May 1882).

[33] *CN*, n° 185, 25 July 1885.

[34] *CN*, n° 190, 29 August 1885.

[35] "Entre deux larrons," *CN*, nouvelle série [from now on, abbreviated in these notes to nvl s.], n° 13, 29 June 1895.

[36] *CN*, n° 54, 20 January 1883. Dedicated to Haraucourt.

[37] *CN*, n° 32, 19 August 1882.

[38] *CN*, n° 46, 25 November 1882; *CN*, n° 49, 16 December 1882; *CN*, n° 52, 6 January 1883.

[39] *CN*, n° 54, 20 January 1883; *CN*, n° 60, 3 March 1883.

[40] *CN*, n° 50, 23 December 1882.

[41] *CN*, n° 55, 27 January 1883.

[42] *Stances et Poèmes* [1865-1866], Paris, Lemerre, 1882, 13-14.

[43] *CN*, n° 660, 15 September 1894.

44 *CN,* n° 597, 1 July 1893.

45 *CN,* n° 4, 4 February 1882.

46 Georges Fragerolle, "Le Fumisme," art. cit.

47 *Id.*

48 Charles Cros, *Le Coffret de santal* [1879], *Œuvres complètes*, Paris, Gallimard, "Bibliothèque de La Pléiade," 1970, p. 138. This monologue in verse was frequently recited in the cabaret by Coquelin Cadet.

49 *CN,* n°166, 14 March 1885.

50 The figure of the elephant moreover takes a greater and greater place in the zoological personnel of *Le Chat Noir*. Faux-Nohain in "Journal de Faux-Nohain de Longcourt (*Année 1896*)" (*CN,* nvl s., n° 62, 5 April 1896), makes this animal the foster brother of the "I": "À cause qu'il est alacre et bon enfant, / J'ai toujours eu un faible pour l'éléphant. / Tout jeune, j'en avais un dans mon berceau, / On lui portait son eau à boire dans un seau." [Because he is joyful and good-natured, / I have always had a weakness for the elephant, / When I was young, I had one in my cradle, / His drinking water was brought in a pail.]

51 For example, Willette leaves in 1889 to found *Le Pierrot*, Marie Krysinska leaves in 1883 and returns in 1890.

52 Charles Cros (1888), Maurice Mac-Nab (1889), and André Gill (1885), to mention only those three.

53 *CN,* n° 21, 3 July 1882.

54 The Incohérents group, headed by Jules Lévy, lasts from 1882 to 1893. Their first exhibits are held at the *Chat Noir* cabaret.

55 Around Cros, who announces its revival in a letter published in the paper (*CN,* n° 84, 18 August 1883).

56 From 25 November 1893 to 10 February 1894. See my article "Mener la vie dure au *Chat Noir*: *La Vie drôle* (novembre 1893-février 1894)," in *Poétique*

du Chat Noir, Caroline Crépiat, Denis, Saint-Amand, Julien Schuh (dir.), Nanterre, Presses Universitaires Paris Nanterre, 2021, 355-366. Also see my chapter on translation (*infra*).

[57] Jules Lemaître, "Préface," *Les Gaîtés du Chat Noir*, Paris, Ollendorff, 1894, 8.

[58] Published every week in *CN*, nvl s., n° 58, 9 May 1896 until the end of the paper (*CN*, nvl s., n° 122, 4 September 1897).

[59] *CN*, n° 124, 24 May 1884.

[60] "As much as or even more than a poet, the good *félibre* is a soldier: by the pen or by the word, by action if necessary, in verse or in prose, in langue d'oc or langue d'oïl, he supports the ideas that are dear to him and fights to defend them." (*CN*, nvl s., n° 59, 16 May 1896).

[61] *CN*, nvl s., n° 58, *op. cit.*

[62] Beginning with *CN*, nvl s., n° 68, 18 July 1896.

[63] Émile Goudeau, "Bulletin littéraire du Chat Noir," *CN*, n° 84, 18 August 1883.

[64] Recurrent insert in the early days of the paper.

[65] Willy, "Fondations littéraires," *CN*, nvl s., n° 121, 24 July 1897.

[66] The editors, "À nos collaborateurs," *CN*, n° 604, 19 August 1893.

[67] *Le Nouveau Chat Noir*, n° 6, 1 August 1900. It is published monthly; the editor in chief is Charles Mahel.

[68] *Id*. Published originally in *CN*, n° 21, 3 June 1882.

CHAPTER TWO
The Reader Has Le Chat Noir's Tongue

[1] We can cite "Hara-Kiri" by Mélandri (*CN*, n° 28, 22 July 1882) which brings in the facetious Alphonse Allais in the role of a coroner, thus acknowledging his pharmaceutical studies and his more general taste for everything concerning the sciences.

[2] [Anonymous], "Charades", *CN*, n° 3, 28 January 1882. The rabbit is a prize for winning such a contest; this vague prize is quickly replaced by a subscription for six months or a year.

[3] Georges Fragerolle, "Le Fumisme," art. cit.

[4] *Id.*

[5] *Id.*

[6] Bernard Sarrazin, "Présentation II," in *L'Esprit fumiste et les Rires fin de siècle,* ed. cit., 35.

[7] Georges Fragerolle, "Le Fumisme," art. cit.

[8] [Jules Jouy], "Casse-tête hebdomadaire," *CN*, n° 138, 30 August 1884.

[9] *CN*, n° 433, 3 May 1890.

[10] *CN*, n° 405, 19 October 1889.

[11] *CN*, n° 41, 21 October 1882.

[12] Willette, "Pierrot s'amuse" [explanatory text for the eponymous picture story], *CN*, n° 60, 3 March 1883.

[13] David Kunzle, "Willette, Steinlen, et les histoires sans paroles du *Chat* Noir," Thierry Groensteen (dir.), *L'humour graphique fin de siècle, Humoresques,* n° 10, Saint-Denis, Presses Universitaires de Vincennes, 1999, 30.

[14] *Ibid.*, 31.

[15] A' Kempis [Émile Goudeau], "Bulletin artistique du *Chat Noir*," *CN*, n°

51, 30 December 1882. Willette refuses at first, but later does it almost systematically.

[16] Numerous amendments and bills are proposed in the 1890s, especially by René Bérenger, nicknamed "Père la Pudeur" [Father Prudery], the president of the Ligue de Défense de la Morale.

[17] From the series "Messe d'amour," *CN* nvl s., n° 42, 18 January 1896.

[18] *CN*, nvl s., n° 112, 22 May 1897.

[19] Jean-Marc Defays, *Jeux et enjeux du texte comique: Stratégies discursives chez Alphonse Allais*, Tübingen, Max Niemeyer Verlag, 1992, 66.

[20] [Jules Jouy], "Casse-tête hebdomadaire," *CN*, n° 127, 14 June 1884.

[21] *Ibid.*, *CN*, n° 128, 21 June 1884.

[22] We note that Alphonse Allais jokes about the illustrious author's passion for riddles by rebaptizing one of his characters with the pun "Poë (de Lapin)" [*peau de lapin*, rabbit skin]. ("Gioventù," *CN*, n° 476, 28 February 1891).

[23] [Jouy J.], "Casse-tête hebdomadaire," *CN*, n° 131, 12 July 1884.

[24] *Ibid.*, *CN*, n° 132, 19 July 1884.

[25] *Ibid.*, *CN*, n° 139, 6 September 1884. In passing, the Abbé Delille's taste for elaborate circumlocution when describing simple things is mocked (see his verses on the snail, for example, in *Trois Règnes de la Nature* (1809)).

[26] *Id.*

[27] *Ibid.*, *CN*, n° 140, 13 September 1884.

[28] *Ibid.*, *CN*, n° 127, *art. cit.*

[29] Émile Boucher, "Avis," *CN*, n° 608, 16 September 1893.

[30] *Id.*

[31] *CN*, n° 611, 7 October 1893. Louis-Gautier (1855-1947) was the student

of the very academic Alexandre Cabanel; a Provençal painter, his work was shown next to Cézanne's. He is mainly known for his landscapes and still lifes.

[32] [The editors], "Nos concours," *CN* nvl s., n° 1, 6 April 1895.

[33] *CN* nvl s., n° 3, 20 April 1895.

[34] Inserted for several weeks beginning with *CN*, n° 317, 4 February 1888.

[35] "Lotte," *CN*, n° 383, 18 May 1889.

[36] *CN* nvl s., n° 60, 23 May 1896.

[37] Willy, "Le *Chat Noir* au Théâtre," *CN*, n° 506, 26 September 1891.

[38] Charles Aubertin, "Les petites chapelles—L'École Symbolisto-Moderniste," *CN*, n° 653, 28 July 1894.

[39] *CN*, n° 616, 11 November 1893.

[40] Gaston Dumestre, "Contes moraux—II Klymnestre," *CN*, n° 630, 17 February 1894.

[41] "Du rôle métaphysique et social des petites annonces," *CN*, n° 684, 2 March 1895.

[42] Bernard Sarrazin, "Présentation II," in *L'Esprit fumiste et les rires fin de siècle*, ed. cit., 36.

[43] *CN*, n° 580, 25 February 1893.

[44] Francisc Sarcé (*alias* Alfons Alè), "La réform de lortograf," *ibid.*

[45] *CN* nvl s., n° 118, 3 July 1897.

[46] The first note is "Word illegible; the writer writes so badly! (Note from the editor)," the second is "Word lost in the typesetting."

[47] "Incroyable étourderie," *CN* nvl s., n° 68, 18 July 1896.

48 Françoise Dubor, *L'Art de parler pour ne rien dire—Le Monologue fumiste fin de siècle*, Rennes, Presses Universitaires de Rennes, coll. "Interférences," 2004, 28.

49 *Ibid.*

50 Lugné-Poe, "Monologue idiot pour faire rire les imbéciles," *CN*, n° 571, 24 December 1892.

51 "Histoires d'Outre-Manche—Le Patron narquois, mais bon au fond—*A Scottish novel*", *CN*, n° 446, 2 August 1890.

52 Quoting Ruckert's verses himself to introduce his chapter about wings (Jules Michelet, *L'Oiseau* [1856], Paris, Hachette, 1867, 87).

53 Willy, "Sauvetage," *CN* nvl s., n° 112, 22 May 1897.

54 Quoted in the epigraph to "Skating," a story by Alphonse Allais (*CN*, n° 317, 4 February 1888).

55 See on this subject Élodie Gaden, "'Gueuler' pour 'écorcher' les règles de l'art. L'humour musical de Marie Krysinska et Maurice Rollinat sur la scène des Hydropathes et du Chat Noir," Journées d'étude des Têtes Chercheuses, Lyon, September 2012, http://teteschercheuses.hypotheses.org/587.

56 Weller S., "Concours pour l'obtention du grade de porteur-hurleur du journal *Le Chat Noir*," *CN* nvl s., n° 46, 15 February 1896.

57 *CN* nvl s., n° 48, 29 February 1896.

58 Faux-Nohain, "Journal de Faux-Nohain de Longcourt," *CN* nvl s., n° 67, 11 July 1896.

59 Nathalie Preiss, "De 'Pouff' à 'Pschitt'!—De la blague et de la caricature politique sous la monarchie de juillet et après…", Philippe Hamon (dir.), *Blague et supercheries littéraires, Romantisme*, n° 116, Paris, SEDES, 2002, 5.

60 Georges Fragerolle, "Le Fumisme," art. cit.

61 *CN* nvl s., n° 51, 21 March 1896.

[62] *Id.*

[63] Seen as a subtitle only on the first seven issues of the paper.

CHAPTER THREE
Fumisme Is Not Just Men's Business!

[1] Émile Goudeau, "Les Hydropathes," *Le Matin*, 13 December 1899. Although he is speaking here about the Club des Hydropathes, it also applies to the cabaret of *Le Chat Noir*.

[2] Jérôme Nau, "Concordances dans l'absurde," *CN*, n° 587, 15 April 1893.

[3] Jules Barbey d'Aurevilly, "Introduction—Du bas-bleuisme contemporain," *Les Œuvres et les hommes*, tome V (1878), éd. Pascale Auraix-Jonchière, in collaboration with Joël Dupont, Pierre Glaudes et Marie-Catherine Huet-Brichard, in Pierre Glaudes, Catherine Mayaux (dir), *Barbey d'Aurevilly—Œuvre critique*, première série - vol. 2, Paris, Les Belles Lettres, 2006, 29.

[4] See Seth Whidden, "'Nous les prendrons, nous les comprendrons'—Une mini-querelle au *Chat Noir*," in *Histoires littéraires, Revue trimestrielle consacrée à la littérature française des XIXe et XXe siècles*, n° 8, vol. II, Tusson, Du Lérot éditeur, October-November-December 2001.

[5] B. Mateu, "Union des femmes peintres et sculpteurs," *CN*, n° 425, 8 March 1890.

[6] Lucien Aressy, *La Dernière bohème, Verlaine et son milieu*, Paris, Jouve et Cie, 1944, 143.

[7] Marie Krysinska, "Les Cénacles artistiques et littéraires. Autour de Maurice Rollinat," *La Revue*, vol. 51, 15 August 1904, 490.

[8] Élodie Gaden, "'Gueuler' pour 'écorcher' les règles de l'art," art. cit.

[9] Marie Krysinska, *La Revue*, art. cit., 490.

[10] Georges Fragerolle, "Le Fumisme," art. cit.

[11] Bernard Sarrazin, "Préface," in *L'Esprit fumiste et les rires fin de siècle, op.*

cit., 30.

[12] *Ibid.*, 35.

[13] Marie Krysinska, "Un poète lyrique—Étude-préface aux œuvres d'Anatole Galureau," *CN*, n° 441, 28 June 1890.

[14] Amélie Villetard, "Sincérités—Rêverie," *CN*, n° 18, 13 May 1882.

[15] For example: "Ballade" (*CN*, n° 46, 25 November 1882), "Chanson d'autrefois" (*CN*, n° 560, 8 October 1892), "Chanson moderne" (*CN*, n° 561, 15 October 1892).

[16] Nina de Villard, "Une Russe," *CN*, n° 55, 27 January 1883.

[17] Marie-Louise Bergeron, "Pour chanter l'amour," *CN*, n° 634, 17 March 1894.

[18] *Op. cit.*

[19] *Op. cit.*

[20] Marie Krysinska, "La Du Barry," *CN*, n° 592, 27 May 1893.

[21] Nina de Villard, *op. cit.*

[22] Jeanne-Thilda, "À une Représentation de Mme de Maintenon à l'Odéon," *CN*, n° 207, 26 December 1885.

[23] *Id.*

[24] Amélie Villetard, "Sincérités—Simple histoire," *CN*, n° 18, 13 May 1882.

[25] Irma Perrot, "Cœur mort," *CN*, n° 634, 17 March 1894.

[26] Marie Krysinska, "Les Bijoux faux," *CN*, n° 77, 30 June 1883.

[27] Charles Maurras, "Le Romantisme féminin," *L'Avenir de la science* (1905), Paris, Nouvelle librairie nationale, 1909, 243.

[28] Amélie Villetard, "Désespoir," *CN*, n° 15, 22 April 1882.

[29] Irma Perrot, "?" *CN*, n° 630, 17 February 1894.

[30] *Op. cit.*

[31] Marie Krysinska, "Bacchanale," *CN*, n° 544, 18 June 1892.

[32] Charles Maurras, art. cit., 250.

[33] Narcisse Lebeau, "*Rythmes pittoresques* par Mme Marie Krysinska," *CN*, n° 457, 18 October 1890.

[34] Marie Krysinska, "Symphonie en gris," *CN*, n° 43, 4 November 1882.

[35] Narcisse Lebeau, art. cit.

[36] For a broader reflection on the situation of women at *Le Chat Noir*, see Marie-Ève Thérenty, "Le beau sesque sur la galère chatnoiresque," in *Poétique du Chat Noir*, ed. cit., 155-168.

PART TWO: THE SUBVERSION OF SERIOUS DISCOURSE

CHAPTER FOUR:
Money

[1] *CN*, n° 48, 9 December 1882.

[2] Em. Moreau-Verneuil, "Petites définitions pour rire," *CN*, nvl s., n° 107, 17 April 1897.

[3] Jean Richepin, "Sonnet consolant," André Velter, *Les Poètes du Chat Noir (anthologie)*, Paris, Gallimard, coll. "Poésie," 1996, 311.

[4] Omega, commenting on "Son Altesse la femme" by Galice, *CN*, n° 375, 23 March 1889.

[5] Adolphe Willette, "Notre-Dame de la Galette," *CN*, n° 106, 19 January 1884.

[6] Jean Lorrain, "Salomé," *CN*, n° 151, 29 November 1884.

[7] Henry D'Erville, "La Crise," *CN*, n° 577, 4 February 1893.

[8] The oxen sing nostalgically about their past glory in "Bœufs gras" by Angelin Ruelle, *CN*, nvl s., n° 101, 6 March 1897.

[9] Albert Glatigny, "Il n'aimait pas le bœuf," *CN*, n° 172, 25 April 1885.

[10] Pimpinelli, "Concerts de cuivres," *CN*, nvl s., n° 3, 20 April 1895.

[11] Boyer d'Agen, "La Litanie du Bourgeois," n° 310, 17 December 1887.

[12] In the picture story "Pierrot a gagné le gros lot" (*CN*, n° 115, 22 mars 1884) by Willette, Pierrot buries 500,000 francs he won in the lottery, but a black cat runs away with his sack of écus.

[13] George Auriol, "Le Coffre-fort," *CN*, n° 449, 23 August 1890.

[14] Maurice Mac-Nab, "Plus de frontières !" *CN*, n° 402, 28 September 1889.

[15] G. Guy-Tong, "Le Calculateur," *CN*, n° 673, 15 December 1894.

[16] Sam Weller, "Nouvel impôt," *CN*, n° 12, nvl s., 22 June 1895.

[17] *CN*, n° 233, 26 June 1886.

[18] *CN*, n° 37, 22 September 1882.

[19] The "Miaulements financiers" (from n° 23, 19 June 1882, to n° 89, 22 September 1883) by Matou, interrupted, from n° 61, 10 March 1883, to n° 71, 19 May 1883 by "*Le Chat Noir* à la Bourse" by Moncrif (who signs the "Miaulements financiers" on their return). From 19 January (n° 106) to 27 December 1884 (n°155), Moncrif's column is entitled "Finances" (then "Finance"), before giving way to a "Bulletin financier" from n° 190, 29 August 1885, to n° 378, 13 April 1889. Following that, n° 433, 3 May 1890, are the "Renseignements financiers," first signed by Baron (Constant) Chanouard, then, after n° 468, 3 January 1891, by L'Échaudé; they end with n° 530, 12 March 1892. From n° 624, 6 January 1894, to n° 664, 13 October 1894, Dom Manuel signs the "Fantaisies financières." "Le Chat Noir financier" continues this endeavor until the penultimate issue of the paper, n° 121, nvl s., 24 July 1897, by turns anonymous or signed by Félin (n° 673, 15 December 1894) or Vodor.

[20] Em. Moreau-Verneuil does not miss the opportunity to make a pun about it (op. cit.): "BONS DE PANAMA (LES)—Épaves jetées à la '*cote*.'" [PANAMA GOODS (THE)—Wrecks washed up on the "stock quote" (with a pun on côte, coast].

[21] Xernand Fau, "Économies," *CN*, n° 161, 7 February 1885. See our chapter on the "little illnesses that one enjoys" (*infra*).

[22] *CN*, n° 106, 19 January 1884.

[23] Dom Manuel, "Fantaisies financières," *CN*, n° 629, 10 February 1894.

[24] Vodor, "Le Chat Noir financier," *CN*, nvl s., n° 3, 20 April 1895.

[25] Ibid., *CN*, nvl s., n° 6, 11 May 1895.

[26] *Id.*

[27] Mon…Crif, "Le Chat Noir à la Bourse," *CN*, n° 61, 10 March 1883.

[28] Matou, "Miaulements financiers," *CN*, n° 26, 8 July 1882.

[29] Ibid., *CN*, n° 25, 1 July 1882.

[30] Ibid., *CN*, n° 35, 9 September 1882.

[31] Ibid., *CN*, n° 32, 19 August 1882.

[32] Ibid., *CN*, n° 23, 19 June 1882.

[33] Daniel Grojnowski, Bernard Sarrazin, op. cit., 274.

[34] "Conte pour rendre les petits enfants fous," *CN*, n° 2, 20 January 1882.

[35] Armand Masson, "Bouchée à la reine," André Velter, op. cit., 257.

[36] Jean Moréas, "Montmartre," *CN*, n° 38, 30 September 1882.

[37] *Id*.

[38] "Maussaderie," *CN*, n° 235, 17 July 1886.

[39] Charles Cros, "À la plus belle," *CN*, n° 146, 25 October 1884.

[40] Émile Goudeau, "Bulletin du Chat Noir," *CN*, n° 107, 26 January 1884.

[41] "Quelques amis," *CN*, n° 461, 15 November 1890.

[42] "La Lune," *CN*, n° 145, 18 October 1884.

[43] Denise speaks of its "metallic brightnesses."

[44] Jean Moréas, op. cit.

[45] *CN*, n° 688, 30 March 1895.

[46] *Charles Baudelaire, Œuvres complètes*, Paris, Gallimard, coll. "Bibliothèque de La Pléiade," 1975, appendix to *Les Fleurs du Mal*, VI. "Bribes," 129.

[47] Paul Marrot, "Nos dieux—Le Dieu jaune," *CN*, n° 97, 17 November 1883.

[48] Charles Aubertin, "Circulaire," *CN*, n° 663, 6 October 1894. This text echoes one by George Auriol ("Manufactures de sonnets," *CN*, n° 374, 8 March 1889).

[49] *Id.*

CHAPTER FIVE

Subverting translation at the end of the 19th century: the examples of two *chatnoiresque* periodicals, *Le Chat Noir* (1882-1897) and *La Vie Drôle* (1893-1894).

[1] Jacques Lehardy [Clément Privé], "Montmartre," *CN*, n° 1, 14 January 1882.

[2] So, Paul Verlaine translated four poems of Arthur Symons, published in *La Revue encyclopédique* (1895), reprinted in *Vers et prose,* in the fascicle of December 1905—January-February 1906; "in addition to!" many translations of Twain, Havelock Ellis and Oscar Wilde (with Henry-D. Davray) published in *Mercure de France*, Gabriel de Lautrec translated Matthew Phipps Shiel for *Je sais tout, magazine encyclopédique illustré* (1911-1912). Only Allais appeared on the first page, twice, with translations of American humorists, especially Mark Twain: "Histoire du petit Stephen Girard," *CN*, n° 454, 27 September 1890, reprinted in *Le Parapluie de l'escouade*, Paris, Ollendorff, 1893.

[3] See our article: "Mener la vie dure au *Chat Noir: La Vie Drôle* (novembre 1893-février 1894)," in *Poétique du Chat Noir*, ed. by Caroline Crépiat, Denis Saint-Amand, Julien Schuh, Presses Universitaires de Paris Nanterre (2021), 355-366.

[4] N. Lorédan, "Sonnet de potache," *CN*, n° 343, 11 August 1888.

[5] Alphonse Allais, "Modernisme," *CN*, n° 176, 23 May 1885.

[6] In fact, what is one to think of the translations, so plentiful, by Henry-D. Davray? Among others.

[7] http://intraduction.huma-num.fr

[8] Alphonse Allais, "Santa Clau's mistake (by gouverneur M. Smith) (Traduit (librement) de l'américain par Alphonse Allais)," illustrations by Henry Somm, *CN*, n° 363, 29 December 1888.

[9] Maurice Curnonsky, "La Chute de l'A privatif," *CN*, n° 682, 16 February 1895.

[10] Alphonse Allais, "Poème morne—Traduit du suisse," *CN*, n° 368, 2 February 1889.

[11] Nathalie Preiss, "De 'Pouff' à 'Pschitt'!—De la blague et de la caricature politique sous la monarchie de juillet et après…", ed. cit., 5.

[12] Alphonse Allais, "Poème morne—Traduit du belge," *Le Parapluie de l'escouade*, Paris, Ollendorff, 1893, 87-93.

[13] Daniel Grojnowski, "Présentation," in *L'Esprit fumiste et les rires fin de siècle*, ed. cit., 10.

[14] Georges Fragerolle, "Le Fumisme," art. cit.

[15] Bernard Sarrazin, "Présentation II," in *L'Esprit fumiste et les rires fin de siècle*, ed. cit., 36.

[16] *CN*, n° 521, 9 January 1892.

[17] Mélandri, "Henry Somm," *CN*, n° 47, 2 December 1882.

[18] *Id.*

[19] Willy, "*Le Chat Noir* au Théâtre", *CN*, n° 573, 7 January 1893. This gives the French text: "Sans conteste, il faut louer l'Ex-Éden de nous donner *Lysistrata*, primo parce que notre ami Donnay regorge de talent, puis parce que son aristophanesque fantaisie inspira à Fernand Vanderem une page éloquente sur le père des Folliculaires comme il l'appelle." [Incontestably, we must praise the Ex-Eden for giving us *Lysistrata*, first because our friend Donni is brimming with talent, and then because his Aristophanic fantasy inspired Fernand Vanderem to an eloquent page on the father of journalists, as he calls him.]

[20] See "The Reader Has the Le Chat Noir's Tongue" (infra).

[21] Jules Jouy, "Casse-tête hebdomadaire," *CN*, n° 138, 30 August 1884.

[22] Willy, "*Le Chat Noir* au Théâtre," *CN*, n° 519, 26 December 1891.

[23] It's Greek, it cannot be translated!

[24] Jean Le Rond D'Alembert, Denis Diderot (dir.), "Transeat," *L'Encyclopédie ou Dictionnaire raisonné des sciences, des arts et des métiers*, t. 16, Neuchâtel, Samuel Faulche, 1751, 546.

[25] In *Le Mercure de France* (1891, t. 3, p. 361-362), Pierre Quillard signs a review of the work published that same year by Tresse et Stock, also resorting to Latin.

[26] "As she broke down in tears, Camille felt wildly excited, she embraced Helen, she glued her mouth to hers, and gasping, joined her body to hers" (Our translation). A month later, this column, with the Latin reworked, is published in *La Plume* (n° 67, 1 February 1892), under the more explicit title of "Lawn-Tennis," but shorn of its *chatnoiresque* punchline. It is no longer a joking matter, no doubt. The version of the scene that appeared in *La Plume* seems even more erotic; among other things, "love" is replaced by "ardor": "Quaedum, insano quodam ardore inflammata ; flebiliter effundit Camilla, Helenam invitam amplectitur, osculum osculo applicat, et cum singultibus, corpori corpus permiscet."

[27] Two birds with one stone, in other words!

[28] Rodolphe Salis, "Simple avis," *CN*, n° 522, 16 January 1892.

[29] But is it really Allais who "signs," or Allais who is saluted? Nothing is less certain: it could also just as well be Auriol, who had taken up the torch for the Captain in *Le Chat Noir* in August 1893—introduced by Allais at the end of 1892—or any other collaborator, to perpetuate this ritual routine launched several months earlier, in the interest of group cohesion. The fact remains that a work by Allais must already have been in process: *Le Captain Cap: ses aventures, ses idées, ses breuvages* was published by Juven in 1902.

[30] [Anonymous], "La Vérité sur *Le Roi des Madrépores*," *La Vie Drôle*, n° 9, 20 January 1894, 7.

[31] "Grand roman psychologique et d'aventure" [Grand Psychological and Adventure Novel] serves as the promotional subtitle of this novel.

[32] He has in fact left Paris, and stays in Nice and in Cannes during December 1893 and January 1894.

[33] Maurice Barrès, "La Querelle des nationalistes et des cosmopolites," *Le Figaro*, 4 July 1892.

[34] They are both active on the very cosmopolitan paper *Paris-Canada*.

[35] Blaise Wilfert-Portal, "La 'querelle du cosmopolitisme' des années 1890—Une perspective socio-historique," in *Romans et récits français, entre nationalisme et cosmopolitisme*, Anne Cadin, Perrine Coudurier, Jessica Desclaux, Marie Gaboriaud, Delphine Nicolas-Pierre (dir.), Paris, Classiques Garnier, coll. "Rencontres," 2017, 90. Transnationalization, a term initially connected to the economy and to neoliberalism, is a political and economic, but also intellectual and cultural, emancipation from territorial logic.

CHAPTER SIX
"Killing Oneself to Amuse Others," or the Mechanisms of Suicide for Laughs

[1] Alphonse Allais, "Sapeck", *CN*, n° 404, 11 October 1889.

[2] The causes are most often alcohol (Charles Cros, 1888), illness (insanity (Sapeck [Eugène Bataille] (1891), André Gill (1885)), cholera, syphilis (one disease among others for Paul Verlaine, 1896), consumption (Maurice Mac-Nab, 1889)), duels (Robert Caze (1886), Harry Alis (1895)), accidents, like an overdose of morphine for Edouard Dubus (1895), etc. Even so, some do commit suicide, but after *Le Chat Noir*: the fittingly named Andhré Joyeux (1899) and Dubut de Laforest (1902). Finally, another makes several attempts, in 1903: Maurice Rollinat.

[3] A' Kempis [Émile Goudeau], "Un Deuil," *CN*, n° 15, 22 April 1882.

[4] Paul Eudel, *Un peu de tout*, Paris, Ollendorff, 1896, cited by Mariel Oberthür, *Le Cabaret du Chat Noir, à Montmartre* (1881-1897), Genève, Slatkine, 2007, 40.

[5] Jean-Pascal, "Histoire mirifique du Chat Noir," *La Musique pour tous*, 3rd year, n° 24, 25 June 1907, 6.

[6] *CN*, n° 16, 29 April 1882.

[7] Steinlen, "Puisqu'ils ne veulent pas se laisser manger, suicidons-les!", *CN*, n° 129, 28 June 1884.

[8] Jean Des Pastèques, "Lettres à nos cousines," *CN*, n° 456, 11 October 1890.

[9] Émile Goudeau, "Chant brutal des viveurs," *CN*, n° 20, 8 July 1882.

[10] L. M., "Notre Dessin," *CN*, n° 44, 11 November 1882.

[11] Émile Goudeau, *Dix ans de bohème* [1888], followed by *Les Hirsutes* by Léo Trézénik, Presentation by Michel Golfier and Jean-Didier Wagneur, Paris, Champ Vallon, 2000, 262.

[12] Jerrold Seigel, Paris-Bohème. *Culture et politique aux marges de la vie bourgeoise (1830-1930)*, Paris, Gallimard, coll. "N. R. F." 1991, 222.

[13] Pimpinelli, "Sage conseil," *CN*, n° 272, 26 March 1887.

[14] *La Confession d'un enfant du siècle*, Paris, Félix Bonnaire, 1836.

[15] Miki, "La Ceinture de Clothilde," *CN*, n° 156, 3 January 1885.

[16] *Toute la Lyre*, Paris, Hetzel & Cie & Maison Quantin, 1888.

[17] "Amour," *Le Livre d'Or du Chat Noir*, Bibliothèque Historique de la Ville de Paris, Ms Res 140, 121.

[18] Sung regularly in the cabaret, and published in the collection *Poèmes incongrus*, Paris, Léon Vanier, 1891, 67.

[19] Charles Baudelaire, "Spleen," *Les Fleurs du Mal, Œuvres complètes*, tome I, Paris, Gallimard, coll. "Bibliothèque de La Pléiade," 1975, 75: "Quand le ciel bas et lourd pèse comme un couvercle." [When the low and heavy sky weighs down like a lid.]

[20] "Spleen," *CN*, n° 100, 8 December 1883.

²¹ André Velter, *Les Poètes du Chat Noir (anthologie)*, Paris, Gallimard, coll. "Poésie/Gallimard," 1996, 310-311.

²² *La Muse à Bibi*, Paris, Marpon et Flammarion, 1881, 54-56.

²³ Le Bocain [picture story], Victor Thiennet [poetry], "Le Cycle volé," *CN*, n° 567, 26 November 1892: "Et se fait passer la colique / Au pied d'un mur mélancolique" [And the diarrhea comes out / At the foot of a melancholy wall.]

²⁴ Suicide symbolizes individual liberty, as Anatole Baju emphasizes: "All the Decadents approve of suicide, but most do not accept that one leave life before being irremediably defeated." ("Décadents et symbolistes," *Le Décadent,* n° 23, 1888).

²⁵ *CN*, nvl s., n° 23, 7 September 1895.

²⁶ "Sensations," *CN*, n° 163, 21 February 1885.

²⁷ "Skating-bière ou l'Asticot de la Providence," *CN*, n° 37, 23 September 1882.

²⁸ Franc-Nohain, "La Romance des romances," *CN*, n° 523, 23 January 1892.

²⁹ Bernard Sarrazin, "Présentation II," in *L'Esprit fumiste et les rires fin-de-siècle,* ed. cit., 36. This is depicted in a wordless picture story by Bombled, "La Leçon de l'expérience" [The Lesson of Experience] (*CN*, n° 344, 18 August 1888): an apprentice woodcutter is sitting on a branch that he is sawing and, inevitably, falls with it.

³⁰ *Id.*

³¹ Albert Lantoine, "Cléopâtre," *CN*, n° 296, 10 September 1887.

³² *CN*, n° 139, 6 September 1884.

³³ The editors, "Evénements de la nuit" [Events of the night], *CN*, n° 42, 28 October 1882: "At the moment that our colleague [Aurélien Scholl] fell, two men stabbed themselves in the heart with a dagger over his bloody corpse. / These men were M. de Dorlodet and M. Paul Bert."

[34] Alphonse Allais, "Pas pressé," *CN*, n° 307, 26 November 1886.

[35] *CN*, n° 164, 28 February 1885.

[36] *Le Dictionnaire historique de la Langue française* (tome I, Paris, 1809, 228) derives this word from the Dutch *balg*, meaning "girdle, envelope," and then "small tobacco sack."

[37] Bernard Sarrazin, "Présentation II," in *L'Esprit fumiste et les rires fin de siècle*, ed. cit., p. 36.

[38] *Les Névroses*, Paris, Charpentier, 1883, p. 259-261.

[39] "Fantasia—II Le pendu bienveillant," *CN*, n° 175, 16 May 1885. According to popular superstition, possessing a bit of rope from a hanged man brings good luck.

[40] *CN*, n° 430, 12 April 1890.

[41] Albert Delvallé, "Volonté," *CN*, n° 420, 1 February 1890.

[42] *CN*, n° 519, 26 December 1891.

[43] *Le Coffret de santal* [1879], *Œuvres complètes*, Paris, Gallimard, "Bibliothèque de La Pléiade," 1970, 138. This monologue in verse is often recited in the cabaret by Coquelin Cadet.

[44] Daniel Grojnowski, *Aux Commencements du Rire moderne—L'Esprit fumiste*, Paris, José Corti, 1997, 51.

[45] *CN*, n° 351, 6 October 1888.

[46] *CN*, n° 140, 13 September 1884.

[47] Mélandri, "Une histoire des temps futurs," *CN*, n° 185, 25 July 1885.

[48] Émile Goudeau, "L'incohérence," *Revue illustrée*, 15 March 1887, 226-233.

[49] Alphonse Allais, "Pour se donner une contenance," *CN*, n° 309, 10 December 1887.

[50] Charles Leroy, "Skating-bière ou l'Asticot de la Providence," op. cit.

[51] Marie Krysinska, "Ronde de printemps," *CN*, n° 383, 18 May 1889.

[52] Daniel Grojnowski, "Présentation," in *L'Esprit fumiste et les rires fin de siècle*, ed. cit., 10.

[53] "L'écosseur de chimères," *CN*, n° 656, 18 August 1894.

[54] *CN*, nvl s., n° 60, 23 May 1896.

[55] Op. cit., 114.

[56] *CN*, n° 148, 8 November 1884.

[57] *CN*, n° 451, 6 September 1890.

[58] Georges Fragerolle, "Le Fumisme," art. cit.

[59] *Id.*

[60] *CN*, n° 117, 5 April 1884.

[61] We can cite "La Veuve," "La Ballade du Guillotiné," "Conseil aux condamnés à mort," "La Complainte de Gamahut"…

[62] Curnonsky, J. Hanisberg, "Le Chat Noir," *Les Œuvres libres*, n° 124, Paris, Fayard, 1956, 188.

[63] *CN*, n° 28, 22 July 1882.

[64] *Hara-Kiri*, Paris, Ollendorff, 1882.

[65] Let us recall that Alphonse Allais began the study of pharmacy.

[66] *CN*, n° 60, 3 March 1883.

[67] *CN*, n° 100, 8 December 1883.

PART THREE: EMBODYING POETIC ECCENTRICITY

CHAPTER SEVEN:
Eroticism

[1] Editor's note [untitled], *CN*, n° 10, 18 March 1882. A paper, whose name is not mentioned, might initiate proceedings against *Le Chat Noir* for this reason.

[2] André Gill, "Le Printemps," *CN*, n° 10, 18 March 1882. Note the date: the anniversary of the Paris Commune.

[3] Raphaël Shoomard, "Mon petit journal," *CN*, n° 560, 8 October 1892.

[4] From 1870 (appointed by Thiers) to 1886.

[5] Henry Salomon, "Ode aux bourgeois," *CN*, nvl s., n° 119, 10 July 1897.

[6] Pierrot, "Les Monstres de Paris—Monsieur Ravaisson, dit Fleur-de-Vigne," *CN*, n° 146, 25 October 1884.

[7] *Id.*

[8] George Auriol, "Le conservateur puni ou la pornographie récompensée," *CN*, n° 146, 25 October 1884.

[9] [Anonymous], "F. P. ?" *CN*, n° 526, 13 February 1892.

[10] *Id.*

[11] *CN*, n° 638, 14 April 1894.

[12] Francisque Sarcey [Alphonse Allais], "Le Bal des Quat'z'arts," *CN*, n° 589, 29 April 1893.

[13] Despite the repression, other events propelling art and the nude into the street will occur several years later, especially in the Vachalcades. See Laurent Bihl, "'L'armée du chahut': les deux vachalcades de 1896 et 1897,"

Sociétés & Représentations 2009/1 (n° 27), 167-191, on line at https://www.cairn.info/revue-societes-et-representations-2009-1-page-167.htm

[14] Francisque Sarcey [Alphonse Allais], "Le Bal des Quat'z'arts," art. cit.

[15] An insert therefore congratulates M. Blot, master typesetter of the rue Bleue, where *Le Chat Noir* is printed, for firing M. Bitard, who "got […] it into his head not to allow anything in our courageous little organ about the Katzar (sic) ball so wittily and sumptuously organized by our friends Henri Guillaume and Jules Roques!" (*CN*, n° 581, 4 March 1893), and announces a *Courrier Français* ball, which will meet, one can guess, a similar fate to the Quat'z'Arts.

[16] Jorge Destèves, "Contes à dormir debout—II Auteur dramatique," *CN*, nvl s., n° 121, 24 July 1897.

[17] And not 1882, as its original cover indicates (Daniel Grojnowski, *La Muse parodique*, Paris, José Corti, 2009, 238), which explains the presence of many of them as early as 1882 in *Le Chat Noir*.

[18] See the chapter "On the Little Illnesses that We Enjoy" (infra).

[19] Stanislas de Guaita, "La Vie et la Mort par Jean Rameau, 1 vol., Giraud, édit., 1886," *CN*, n° 220, 27 March 1886.

[20] [The editors], "La Chanson des étoiles par Jean Rameau," *CN*, n° 335, 16 June 1888.

[21] *Id.*

[22] Cf. The title of his collection, *La Chanson des étoiles* (1888).

[23] Jean Rameau, "Prière au Soleil," *CN*, n° 316, 28 January 1888.

[24] Jean Rameau, "La Planète d'Amour," *CN*, n° 265, 5 February 1887.

[25] Phillip Dennis Cate, "'Le Louvre de Montmartre' et l'École du Chat Noir" (translated by Caroline Crépiat), in *Poétique du Chat Noir*, Caroline Crépiat, Denis Saint-Amand, Julien Schuh (dir.), Presses Universitaires de Paris Nanterre, 2021, 30.

26 Edmond Haraucourt, "La Jeune (Sonnet)," *CN*, n° 48, 9 December 1882.

27 *CN*, n° 25, 1 July 1882: "sous le voile blanc [elles] portent leur propre deuil" [under the white veil [they] wear their own mourning].

28 *CN*, n° 45, 18 November 1882.

29 Edmond Haraucourt, "La Jeune (Sonnet)," *op. cit.*: "enfant" [child]; Charles Cros, "Vision," *CN*, n° 123, 17 May 1884: "fraîche fillette" [fresh little girl]; and Alphonse Allais, "Sur le vif," *CN*, n° 224, 24 April 1886: "moitié baby, moitié jeune fille" [half baby, half girl].

30 Numa Blès, "Ballade à la Lune," *CN*, nvl s. n° 47, 22 February 1896.

31 Alfred Clauzel, "La neige à Paris," *CN*, n° 165, 7 March 1885.

32 Maurice Rollinat, *L'Abîme*, Paris, Charpentier & Cie, 1886, 115-116.

33 Louis Denise, "Figulines parisiennes," *CN*, n° 184, 18 July 1885.

34 Pierre Guiraud, *Le Langage de la sexualité tome I, Dictionnaire historique, stylistique, rhétorique, étymologique de la littérature érotique*, Paris, Payot, 1978, 174. See the poem "La Blanchisseuse du Paradis" by Maurice Rollinat (*Les Névroses*, Fasquelle, 1917, 47).

35 Alfred Clauzel, "La neige à Paris," *op. cit.*

36 Maurice Rollinat, *op. cit.*

37 Edmond Haraucourt, "La Jeune (Sonnet)," *op. cit.*

38 *Op. cit.*

39 Georges Jéhel, "Réponse," *CN*, nvl s., n° 112, 22 May 1897.

40 Poem excerpted from *Déliquescences—Poèmes décadents d'Adoré Floupette, avec sa vie par Marius Tapora* (Byzance [Paris], Lion Vanné [Léon Vanier], 1885), published in an article by Louis Marsolleau, "Adoré Floupette" (*CN*, n° 177, 30 May 1885).

[41] To be admired at the Musée Carnavalet, in Paris.

[42] *CN*, nvl série n° 47, 22 February 1896. This ballad is inspired by Musset's poem of the same name, also about a wedding night, but which goes badly: the husband senses a troublesome presence, which is none other than the moon watching them.

[43] The *jambages* (downstrokes) recall the *droit de jambage* (synonym for the *droit du seigneur*).

[44] Pierre Guiraud, op. cit., 505 : pen means penis.

[45] "S'échauffe" (*ibid.*, 196: "to have an erection"), "s'élargissent," "s'allongent" (*ibid.*, 132: "to have a hard-on"), "s'étalent" (*ibid.*, 318: *étaller* = to copulate), "court" which also means to copulate.

[46] Ferdinand Loviot, "Romance," *CN*, nvl s., n° 56, 25 April 1896.

[47] Edmond Haraucourt, *La Légende des Sexes—Poëmes hystériques, op. cit.*, 59 : "Là… vite! Plus longtemps! / Je fonds! Attends / Oui… Je t'adore… // Va! Va! Va! / Encore! / Ha!" [There… quick! Longer! / I'm melting! Wait / Yes… I adore you… // Go! Go! Go! / Again! Ha!"

[48] *CN*, n° 123, 17 May 1884.

[49] Edmond Haraucourt, "Ballade des pucelaiges morts," *op. cit.*

[50] *Le Chat Noir*, n° 45, 18 November 1882.

[51] *CN*, n° 624, 6 January 1894.

[52] Catherine Dousteyssier-Khoze, "Fumisme: le rire jaune du Chat Noir," in *Abnormalities,* Catherine Dousteyssier-Khoze, Paul Scott (dir.), Durham, Durham Modern Languages Series, 2001, 151.

[53] L. Henseling, "Musique de chambre," *CN*, nvl s., n° 57, 2 May 1896: the young woman's "rippling laugh."

[54] *CN*, n° 27, 15 July 1882.

[55] Pierre Guiraud, *op. cit.*, 552.

[56] Charles Cros, "Le Caillou mort d'amour—Histoire tombée de la lune," *CN*, n° 219, 20 March 1886.

[57] *CN*, n° 28, 22 July 1882.

[58] Dubut de Laforest, "Les Vierges contemporaines," *CN*, n° 30, 5 August 1882.

[59] Edmond Haraucourt, "La Jeune (Sonnet)," op. cit.

[60] Bénoni Glador, "Dégrafée," *CN*, n° 442, 5 July 1890.

CHAPTER EIGHT
Chamber Pots, Enemas, and Cannulas

[1] Léon Bloy, "Le fond des cœurs," *CN*, n° 143, 4 October 1884.

[2] *Id.*

[3] We refer to the online version: http://www.cnrtl.fr/definition/intime.

[4] Gérard Legrand, *Dictionnaire de philosophie*, Paris, Bordas, 1983.

[5] *CN*, n° 537, 30 April 1892.

[6] George Auriol, "Un amateur," *CN*, n° 250, 23 October 1886.

[7] A' Kempis [Émile Goudeau], "Un Deuil," *CN*, n° 15, 22 April 1882.

[8] *Id.*

[9] Adolphe Willette, "Pierrot attristé," *CN*, n° 19, 20 May 1882.

[10] *Id.*

[11] Rodolphe Salis, "Messer Satanas dans le Drageoir aux Cholliques," *CN*, n° 139, 6 September 1884.

[12] *Le Trésor de la Langue Française*: http://www.cnrtl.fr/lexicographie/drageoir.

¹³ A drageoir is used, as the name indicates, to hold "dragées and other confections." (*id.*).

¹⁴ Lucien Rigaud, *Dictionnaire du jargon parisien—L'argot ancien et l'argot moderne* (1878), new edition with supplement, Paris, Ollendorff, 1888, 244.

¹⁵ *Ibid.*, 314.

¹⁶ Remember these lines from "Sonnet du trou du cul" by Rimbaud and Verlaine: "C'est le tube où descend la céleste praline" [It is the tube where the celestial praline descends].

¹⁷ Rodolphe Salis, "Comment fust le sieur Jehan Faulcon piteusement desbouté par une oiselière qui avoit nom Blanche," André Velter, *Les Poètes du Chat Noir (anthologie)*, ed. cit., 85-87.

¹⁸ Lucien Rigaud, *op. cit.*, 48.

¹⁹ Quoted in André Velter, *op. cit.*, 171-173.

²⁰ Charles Virmaître, *Dictionnaire d'argot fin-de-siècle*, Preface by Léo Trézenik, Paris, A. Charles Libraire, 1894, 95.

²¹ *CN*, n° 14, 15 April 1882.

²² The carnivalesque is "marked especially by putting the original sense of things 'upside down,' 'on the contrary,' by constant permutations of the high and the low ("the wheel"), the face and the buttocks." (Mikhaïl Bakhtine, *L'Œuvre de François Rabelais et la culture populaire au Moyen-Âge et sous la Renaissance*, Paris, Gallimard, coll. "Tel," 1970, 19).

²³ Daniel Grojnowski, "Présentation," in *L'Esprit fumiste et les rires fin de siècle*, ed. cit., 10.

²⁴ Doës, "Intempestive substitution" [wordless picture story], *CN*, n° 333, 2 June 1888.

²⁵ Godefroy, "Intermède" [wordless picture story], *CN*, n° 340, 21 July 1888.

²⁶ Moïse Renault [Rodolphe Salis ?], "Le Bayser perfeumé—Comment le

sire de Continvoir voulust bayser le visaige d'ugne pucelle et le treuva non tel que cuydoyt (Suite et fin)," *CN*, n° 302, 22 October 1887. In this story, after a prank by his servants, Continvoir is taken "de male paour, et par relaschement anal causé par lez clystères, avoyt conchié toutes ses chausses des genoils iusques à la braguette, ce qui n'estoyt qu'ordeure et villenye" [with terrible fear, and due to the anal relaxation caused by the enemas, had beshitted his pantaloons from the knees to the codpiece, which was nothing but ordure and villainy].

[27] Adolphe Willette, "Pierrot attristé," *op. cit.* The coffin that awaits Pierrot is in fact set next to five chamber pots: the black fumes rising from them add to the parallel.

[28] *CN*, n° 32, 19 August 1882.

[29] Roger-Henri Guerrand, *Les Lieux—Histoire des commodités* (1985), Paris, La Découverte, 1997, 78.

[30] "It is recommended that one purge oneself at least once a week," says an ad for the purgative Géraudel, to which the paper devotes a whole page (*CN*, n° 444, 19 July 1890).

[31] *Id.*

[32] Alphonse Allais, "Le Railleur puni," *CN*, n° 260, 1 January 1887.

[33] Fernand Fau, "Dessin," *CN*, n° 292, 13 August 1887.

[34] Victor Hugo, "Préface," *Odes et Ballades* [1822], *Œuvres complètes*, Paris, Ollendorff, 1912, 5.

[35] *CN*, n° 264, 29 January 1887.

[36] Léon Bloy, art. cit.

[37] Victor Hugo, "Fonction du poète," *Les Rayons et les Ombres, Œuvres complètes,* Paris, Ollendorff, 1909, 540.

[38] Charles Baudelaire, "Victor Hugo," *Réflexions sur quelques uns de mes contemporains* (1861), *Œuvres complètes*, ed. Claude Pichois, tome II, Paris, Gallimard, coll. "Bibliothèque de La Pléiade," 1975, 133.

[39] Arthur Rimbaud, letter to Georges Izambard, May 1871, *Œuvres complètes*, ed. André Guyaux, Aurélia Cervoni, Paris, Gallimard, coll. "Bibliothèque de La Pléiade," 2009, 340.

[40] This is the title Piero Lorenzoni gives his work: *La giuliva siringa: storia universale del clistere*, Milan, Edizioni del Borghese, 1969.

[41] *CN*, n° 328 bis, 28 April 1888.

[42] Let us point out that this poem is dedicated to Alphonse Allais, who studied pharmacy.

[43] Often recited at *Le Chat Noir*, quoted by André Velter, op. cit., 340-341.

[44] Mikhaïl Bakhtine, *op. cit.*

CHAPTER NINE
"Let Us Be Fine Chiselers of Turds"? On the Art of "Making" Well

[1] Jean des Deubourneau, "Mélancolie," *CN*, n° 284, 18 June 1887.

[2] Jules Jouy, *Les Lamentations de Jules Simon*, quoted on an untitled drawing by Saint-Maurice, *CN*, n° 537, 30 April 1892.

[3] "It is recommended that one purge oneself at least once a week," we are told in an ad for Géraudel lozenges (*CN*, n° 444, 19 July 1890).

[4] *Id.*

[5] *Id.*

[6] One of these papers is devoted entirely to the subject: *Le Journal des merdeux*, whose only issue appears in April 1882. Jules Jouy, one of the singers at *Le Chat Noir*, is the editor.

[7] *Op. cit.*

[8] Mikhaïl Bakhtine, *L'Œuvre de François Rabelais et la culture populaire au Moyen-Âge et sous la Renaissance*, ed. cit.

⁹ Especially since, it must be remembered, *Le Chat Noir* is also a weekly.

¹⁰ Georges Fragerolle, "Le Fumisme," art. cit.

¹¹ *Le Littré*: "rendre des excréments" [to produce excrement].

¹² Lucien Rigaud, *Dictionnaire du jargon parisien,* ed. cit., 160. It is a question here of the first meaning of the verb *faire* (and therefore the most used), which is given nine here, not counting the derived expressions.

¹³ Daniel Grojnowski, "Présentation," in *L'Esprit fumiste et les rires fin de siècle,* ed. cit., 18.

¹⁴ *Ibid.,* 10.

¹⁵ *CN,* n° 215, 20 February 1886.

¹⁶ Hercule is the antihero par excellence; his expected Herculean strength is transferred to this "uncommon" water, which leads him to think only in commonplaces, to lose the first syllable of his name and become a *cul* (ass).

¹⁷ Le Bocain [picture story], Victor Thiennet [poetry], "Le Cycle volé," *CN,* n° 567, 26 November 1892: "Et se fait passer la colique / Au pied d'un mur mélancolique" [And the diarrhea comes out / At the foot of a melancholy wall.]

¹⁸ Comedy in one act, performed for the first time 25 December 1885, published and sold at *Le Chat Noir.*

¹⁹ His strategy is essentially the same Hercule's, mentioned above.

²⁰ *Id.,* 15: "A constipated man seems to me in every way the son-in-law of my dreams. Léocadie will only marry a constipated man, with whom no noise will trouble the intimacy of our home, for, except for our commercial connections, we shall see few people; inside is where we want to live! […] You are, it is true, handsome, young, brilliant, but you are not constipated!…"

²¹ To quote the leitmotiv of the song by Bakouk, the servant (*Id.,* 18).

²² Daniel Grojnowski, *Aux commencements du rire moderne—L'esprit*

fumiste, ed. cit., 51

[23] "—Mes étrennes, Monsieur ! c'est moi qui suis votre aimable vidangeur…" *CN*, n° 564, 5 November 1892.

[24] L. Henséling, "Cas de conscience," *CN*, nvl s., n° 86, 21 November 1896. Les note that in slang, "conscience" (Lucien Rigaud, *op. cit.*, 109) means "belly, stomach."

[25] L. Henséling, "Cas de conscience," *op. cit.*

[26] A guest, behind the screen in his hosts' bedroom (Godefroy, "Intermède," *CN*, n° 340, 21 July 1888).

[27] *CN*, n° 333, 2 June 1888.

[28] Franc-Nohain, in "La Romance des romances" (*CN*, n° 523, 23 January 1892), uses this expression to challenge the originality of Marie Krysinska's writing, repeating Barbey d'Aurévilly's argument ("Introduction—Du bas-bleuisme contemporain," ed. cit.), according to which the woman poet imitates men instead of creating: "Copier du Sully-Prudhomme / Sur des albums verts, très verts ; / Et prouver que l'on est un homme, / En faisant des vers, des vers." [Copying Sully-Prudhomme / In albums that are green, very green; / And proving that one is a man, / By making verses, verses.]

[29] Charles Aubertin, "Rodolphe Salis et l'évolution littéraire," *CN*, n° 669, 17 November 1894.

[30] "Manufacture de sonnets" (Georges Auriol, art. cit.) describes, in the style of a newspaper report, a visit to such a business: "We immediately pass into the *Hall of sonnets on demand*. It is staffed by extremely skillful workers who can create in less than five minutes sonnets on any subject […]; some virtuosos are even able to compose two or three sonnets at the same time."

[31] Ogier d'Ivry, "Décadisme," *C N*, n° 284, 18 June 1887.

[32] As an epigraph.

[33] Alias Léopold Dauphin.

[34] *CN*, nvl s., n° 16, 20 July 1895.

[35] *CN*, nvl s., n° 112, 22 May 1897.

[36] *Id.*

[37] *Id.*

[38] Publisher of medical works (1828-1883). The writer alludes here to certain of its publications, like *Des hémorroïdes et de la chute du rectum* by Almire René Jacques Lepelletier (1834) or *De l'âge critique chez les femmes, des maladies qui peuvent survenir à cette époque de la vie, et des moyens de les combattre et de les prévenir* by Charles Menville (1840), one of whose chapters is devoted to "hemorrhoids and hemorrhoidal flux."

[39] Michel Campi, "Et patati et patata!" *CN*, n° 119, 19 April 1884.

[40] *Op. cit.* To be noted: in Old French a bournel is a water pipe.

[41] Pierre Schappel, "Dolence d'être," *CN*, n° 318, 11 February 1888. It is a question here of precursors to the act (cf. Rigaud, op. cit., 26: *ballon* [ball] means *derrière*). Let us also quote the final lines of "Contes immoraux—I La Vengeance du mort" (Gaston Dumestre, *CN*, n° 626, 20 January 1894) whose suspension points are interrupted by the onomatopoeia "Pfutt!" that replaces them: ". ". . . . . / Pfutt!... Pfutt..... Pfutt! Pfutt! Pfutt! Pfutt!... / Gently, the dead deflate, polluting the air. / The sleeping man suffocates bit by bit. / […] Then, the drowned man seats himself and contemplates him, ironically, then, lying on his back again, bursts out laughing on seeing that the guard, who is deflating in turn, has blown out the little blue flame with his first pfutt!..." We are also reminded of "L'Expulsion" by Maurice Mac-Nab (published in his *Poèmes incongrus* (op. cit., 13-15), but whose version given by Charles Virmaître (*Dictionnaire d'argot fin-de-siècle*, ed. cit., 121) is more interesting to us): ". . . . . / Il reste les Napoléon, / Des muff's qu'a toujours la colique / Et qui foire dans ses pantalons / Pour em…bêter la République." [There are still the Napoleons, / Boors who always have diarrhea / And who mess their pants / To annoy the Republic (*em…bêter* is suspended to suggest the more vulgar *emmerder*)]

[42] Charles Virmaître, *ibid.*, 66: "writers."

[43] Rigaud and Virmaître both define the "comma" with humor:

"Excremental punctuation that coats the walls of certain public latrines. Attempts at impressionist painting done by hoodlums on the walls of these establishments." (Lucien Rigaud, *op. cit.*, 387); "In almost all the comfort stations in populous houses and studios, on the wall there are commas that are so many signatures of the swine who pass through there." (Charles Virmaître, *op. cit.*, p. 311-312).

[44] Lucien Rigaud, *ibid.*

[45] We borrow this term from the poem "Les Angoisses" by Franc-Nohain (*CN*, n° 565, 12 November 1892), whose leitmotiv stresses the implacable aspect of the *bifur*.

[46] *CN*, n° 72, 26 May 1883.

[47] Georges Fragerolle, "Le Fumisme," art. cit.

[48] *CN*, n° 649, 30 June 1894.

[49] This is obviously a parody of "Ce que dit la Bouche d'ombre" by Victor Hugo.

[50] Daniel Grojnowski, "Le rire 'moderne' à la fin du XIXe siècle," *Poétique*, n° 84, Paris, Le Seuil, November 1990, 462.

[51] The reader may recall these verses from the "Sonnet du trou du cul": "la flûte câline ; / C'est le tube où descend la céleste praline." [the affectionate flute; / It is the tube where the celestial praline descends.]

[52] Maurice Mac-Nab, "Le Clysopompe," Often recited in the cabaret, cited in André Velter, *Les Poètes du Chat Noir (anthologie)*, ed. cit., 340-341.

[53] *CN*, nvl s., n° 118, 3 July 1897.

[54] As Georges Fragerolle points out ("Le Fumisme," art. cit.): "To be a good fumiste, it is often indispensable to be a lion wearing an ass's skin"; an ass's skin, in slang, means a drum (Lucien Rigaud, *Dictionnaire du jargon parisien*, ed. cit., 252).We thus have the image of an instrument that is certainly loud, but filled with air, with emptiness, and is above all deceptive.

[55] "Le Cor," *Poèmes antiques et modernes* (1826), *Poésies complètes*, Paris,

Michel Lévy frères, 1866, 147-152.

[56] Note the parallel construction ("son de votre douce voix," "son du corps sous les doigts").

[57] Cf. Jules Laforgue and his poetic art: "To make something original at all costs." (Letter of 14 May 1883, *Œuvres complètes*, Lausanne, L'Âge d'Homme, 2000, t.1, 821).

[58] Daniel Grojnowski, *Aux commencements du rire moderne—L'esprit fumiste*, ed. cit., 245.

[59] *CN*, n° 276, 23 April 1887.

[60] Armand Masson, "Spiritualisme," *CN*, n° 54, 20 January 1883.

[61] Jules Jouy, "L'Album de M. Jules Grévy," *CN*, n° 216, 27 February 1886.

[62] A metaphor at the time for the toilet, repeated in *La Berline de l'émigré*, "WC" by George Auriol (*CN*, n° 448, 16 August 1890) etc.

[63] Émile Goudeau, "Bulletin littéraire du Chat Noir," *CN*, n° 84, 18 August 1883. More precisely, not to put oneself "behind the shadow of a great man."

CHAPTER TEN
On the Little Illnesses That We Enjoy

[1] Georges Lorin, "Rivale!" *CN*, n° 512, 7 November 1891.

[2] Maurice Mac-Nab, "Plus de cor!" *Poèmes mobiles—Monologues*, Paris, Vanier, 1886, 11-13.

[3] Notably Le Bocain (drawing), Victor Thiennet (poetry), "Le Cycle volé," *CN*, n° 567, 26 November 1892.

[4] B. Pétris, "Rhumatismes," *CN*, nvl s., n° 52, 28 March 1896.

[5] Bernard Sarrazin, "Présentation II," in *L'Esprit fumiste et les rires fin de siècle*, ed. cit., 36.

[6] Schematization also goes in the opposite direction: epidemics are also

invoked, especially cholera, but personified in a way that detracts from any individual depiction of their victims. So, in a prose poem by George Auriol ("Ballade du joyeux Choléra," *CN*, n° 149, 15 November 1884), cholera is called "joyful," "gallops through space," and shows itself preoccupied above all with competing with the plague in its hours of glory.

[7] Sam Weller, "L'Avis littéraire," *CN* nvl s., n° 53, 4 April 1896.

[8] Georges Lorin, "Rivale!" op. cit.

[9] To use the title of Stéphane Mallarmé's famous essay, published in 1895.

[10] Camille de Sainte-Croix, "Les Complices," *CN*, n° 213, 6 February 1886.

[11] Raoul Ponchon, "La Salade," *La Muse au Cabaret* [1920], Paris, Grasset et Fasquelle, 1998, 165. This collection, the only one published in his lifetime, includes a certain number of poems written in the 1880s.

[12] Cf. Mikhaïl Bakhtine, *L'Œuvre de François Rabelais et la culture populaire au Moyen-Âge et sous la Renaissance*, ed. cit.

[13] Léo Niversac, "Bulletin du Chat Noir," *CN*, n° 129, 28 June 1884.

[14] Gaston Dumestre, "Les Macchabés," *CN*, n° 610, 30 September 1893.

[15] J. Derriaz, "Le Printemps," *CN*, n° 67, 21 April 1883.

[16] Xernand Fau, "Économies," *CN*, n° 161, 7 February 1885.

[17] Maurice Curnonsky, "Interview de Cornélius Herz," *CN*, n° 612, 14 octobre 1893. The text is even more flavorful because Curnonsky later makes a career as a culinary critic. His works on gastronomy are still standard references.

[18] *Id.*

[19] This is the scientific term used by Victor Treille in particular, in his *Étude sur le ver solitaire ou les ténias armés, ténias inermes, etc. Le bothriocéphale, les oxyures et les ascarides lombrocoïdes* (1875), Paris, Baillière et Fils, 1906.

[20] [Anonymous], "Singulier cas," *CN*, n° 499, 8 August 1891.

[21] Gaston Dumestre, "Contes moraux III—Les deux vers solitaires," *CN*, n° 632, 3 March 1894.

[22] Victor Treille showed that "several can exist in the same individual, and simultaneously with certain other worms" (op. cit., 15). The teniafuge that he perfected permitted "M. S… of Saint-Étienne to evacuate 17 armored tapeworms, each with its head. This fact, although it appears supernatural, is authentic and legally certified." (*id.*).

[23] Gaston Dumestre, *op. cit.*

[24] These characteristics are noted and described by Nathalie Prince in *Les Célibataires du fantastique—Essai sur le personnage célibataire de la littérature fantastique de la fin du XIXe siècle*, Paris, L'Harmattan, coll. "Critiques Littéraires," 2002. We can cite as examples: Des Esseintes (Joris-Karl Huysmans, À rebours (1884)), D'Entragues (Remy de Gourmont, Sixtine, roman de la vie cérébrale (1890)) and later, the Duc de Fréneuse (Jean Lorrain, Monsieur de Phocas (1901)).

[25] Edmond and Jules de Goncourt, Charles Demailly [1860], *Œuvres complètes*, Genève/Paris, Slatkine Reprints, 1986, t. VIII-IX, 243.

[26] Nathalie Prince, *op. cit.*, 29.

[27] [Anonymous], "Singulier cas," op. cit. It is an amusing way to imagine the tapeworm's hermaphroditism.

[28] Gaston Dumestre, "Contes moraux V—Glabre-Éphèbe fils," *CN*, n° 638, 14 April 1894.

[29] André Barre, *Le Symbolisme: essai historique sur le mouvement poétique en France de 1885 à 1900*, Paris, Jouve, 1911, 68.

[30] *Id.*

[31] For the detailed account of this battle, see among others Clive Scott, *Vers libre—The Emergence of Free Verse in France (1886-1914)*, Oxford, Clarendon, 1990, and Florence R. J. Goulesque, *Une femme symboliste, Marie Krysinska—La Calliope du* Chat Noir, Paris, Honoré Champion, 2001.

[32] Adoré Floupette, "Pizzicatti," quoted in an article by Louis Marsolleau,

"Adoré Floupette," *CN*, n° 177, 30 May 1885.

[33] *CN*, n° 37, 23 September 1882.

[34] [Georges Camuset], *Les Sonnets du Docteur* (1884), Dijon, Les Éditions du Raisin, 1926, 7.

[35] Vincent Hyspa, "Le Ver solitaire," *Chansons d'Humour*, Paris, Énoch et Cie, 1903, 297-303.

[36] Alfred Béjot, "Dzim! Boum! Symboles!", *CN*, n° 610, 30 September 1893.

[37] Henri Galoy, "Chanson bancale," *CN* nvl s., n° 120, 17 July 1897.

[38] Jean de Palacio, *La Décadence—Le Mot et la Chose*, Paris, Les Belles Lettres, coll. "Essais," 2011, 140.

[39] Alfred Béjot, *op. cit.*

[40] Marc Angenot, "La poésie socialiste au temps de la Deuxième Internationale," *Discours social,* vol. 33, Montréal, Chaire James McGill, a study on the social discourse, 7.

[41] *Ibid.*, p. 10. One might add advertising. It is, for example, in the form of an "Acrostiche hygiénique" that Cusenier absinthe is praised (*CN*, n° 304, 5 November 1887), and there are six verses on the phosphated wine Tarible, "À l'hémoglobine et à la kola" (*CN* nvl s., n° 55, 18 April 1896).

[42] For example in Édouard Norès, "Microbes," *CN*, n° 352, 13 October 1888 and Jules Saint-Honoré, "Le Microbe," *CN*, n° 629, 10 February 1894.

[43] Jules Saint-Honoré, *id.*

[44] *Id.*

[45] Charles Aubertin, "Le Symbolisme devant la science," *CN*, n° 676, 5 January 1895.

[46] Félix Arvers, *Mes heures perdues* (1833).

[47] Among the parodists, we can cite Jules Renard, Tristan Bernard, and even

Raoul Ponchon.

[48] Victor Hugo, "Le Sonnet d'Arvers… à revers," Jean-Paul Goujon, *Anthologie de la poésie érotique française*, Paris, Fayard, 2004, 731-732.

[49] *CN*, n° 673, 15 December 1894.

[50] Quoted in Louis Marsolleau, "Adoré Floupette," op. cit.

[51] Vincent Hyspa, "Le Ver solitaire," op. cit.

[52] [The editors], "Goguette du Chat Noir," *CN*, n° 526, 13 February 1892.

[53] Maurice Donnay, in the preface he writes for Hyspa's collection *Chansons d'humour, op. cit.*, 9-10.

[54] *Ibid.*, 10.

[55] *Id.*

[56] Ferdinand Loviot, "Sonnet-Réponse," *CN*, n° 453, 20 September 1890, dedicated to Gaston Dumoraize.

[57] Pimpinelli, "À Émile Boucher," *CN* nvl s., n° 9, 1 June 1895.

[58] Émile Boucher, "À Pimpinelli", *CN* nvl s., n° 10, 8 June 1895.

[59] Syllepsis is a stylistic device that consists of using a single signifier to refer to two signifieds; usually, the same word is taken in both its literal and figurative meanings. Dominique Noguez makes it the major device in humor; see especially *L'Arc en ciel des humours* (2000).

[60] Albert Samain, "Biscuit," *CN*, n° 176, 23 May 1885.

ACKNOWLEDGMENTS
(continued from copyright page)

"Du rire de l'argent au fumisme de l'or poétique dans la revue du *Chat Noir* - Pour un décentrement fantaisiste du rire du texte par le motif de l'argent" appeared in *L'Argent et le Rire au XIXe siècle de Balzac à Mirbeau*, Florence Fix, Marie-Ange Fougère (ed.), Rennes, Presses Universitaires de Rennes (2012).

"Drôles de traductions – Subvertir la traduction à la fin du XIXe siècle : *Le Chat Noir* (1882-1897)" and "Drôles de traductions – Une parodie de la circulation médiatique des traductions : *La Vie Drôle* (1893-1894)" appeared in *Melliflux décadent*, online (2020) ; to be published in *Amer fanzine*, 3, Lille, Les Âmes d'Atala (2021).

"'Se tu[er] à amuser les autres' ou les mécanismes du suicide pour rire au *Chat Noir* (1882-1897)" appeared in *Suicide : question sociétale ou individuelle ?*, Grégory Bouchaud, Caroline Crépiat, Gheorghe Derbac, Alice Juliet, Anaïs Gayte-Papon de Lameigné (ed.), Clermont-Ferrand, Michel de L'Hospital (2018).

"'Rayonne[r] dans les nues' - L'érotisme des planètes chez Jean Rameau" appeared in *Amer, revue finissante*, 8, *NU - Effeuillage littéraire*, Lille, Les Âmes d'Atala (2018) ; and "Pour un fumisme du dire érotique dans la revue du *Chat Noir* – L'exemple du contre-chant de la virginité", conference done during *Doctoriales I : Écritures de l'érotisme*, Clermont-Ferrand (2012).

"Pots de chambre, clystères et canules dans la revue *Le Chat Noir*" appeared in *Sociopoétique* [online], *Mythes, contes et sociopoétique* (2016).

"'Soyons fins ciseleurs d'étrons' ? – De l'art de bien *faire* dans *Le Chat Noir*" appeared in *Amer, Revue finissante*, 6, *Monstre végétal – Écologie de l'imaginaire*, Lille, Les Âmes d'Atala (2014).

"Des petites maladies qu'on déguste dans *Le Chat Noir*" appeared in *Amer, Revue finissante*, 7, *Bouffe, Gastrosophie littéraire*, Lille, Les Âmes d'Atala (2016).

ABOUT THE AUTHOR

Caroline Crépiat completed a PhD on the lyric subject in the poems published in *Le Chat Noir* (2016). Her research works focus on the relationship between fin-de-siecle press and literature, humor, women authors, and the topic of the body. She frequently contributes fin-de-siecle nonsense to *Black Scat Review*. She co-edited with L. Lavergne *Masques, corps, langues – Les figures dans la poésie érotique contemporaine* (2017) ; with G. Bouchaud, G. Derbac, A. Gayte, A. Juliet *Le suicide – Question individuelle ou sociétale ?* (2018); *Poétique du Chat Noir*, with J. Schuh and D. Saint-Amand (2021).

ABOUT THE TRANSLATOR

Doug Skinner has translated many works by writers from fin-de-siècle Paris, including Alphonse Allais, Alfred Jarry, Charles Cros, and Émile Goudeau. He has also contributed to many magazines, worked for decades in the theater, and done other interesting things.

2 + 2 = 5 Alphonse Allais
NO BILE! Alphonse Allais
DOUBLE OVER Alphonse Allais
THE BLAIREAU AFFAIR Alphonse Allais
CAPTAIN CAP Alphonse Allais
LONG LIVE LIFE! Alphonse Allais
MASKS: DELUXE SPECIAL EDITION Alphonse Allais
PINK AND APPLE GREEN Alphonse Allais
THE SQUADRON'S UMBRELLA Alphonse Allais
I AM SARCEY Alphonse Allais
THE ALPHONSE ALLAIS READER
SELECTED PLAYS OF ALPHONSE ALLAIS
HIDDEN GEMS: THE BEST OF *THE PEARL* Anonymous
THE ZOMBIE OF GREAT PERU Pierre-Corneille de Blessebois
SMELLS LIKE TEEN 'PATAPHYSICS Norman Conquest
COLLECTED MONOLOGUES Charles Cros
UPSIDE-DOWN STORIES Charles Cros
EROTIC TALES Catherine D'Avis
FROM THEIR LIPS TO HIS EARS Denis Diderot
TODAY IS THE DAY THAT WILL MATTER Debra Di Blasi
THE PISSERS' THEATRE Eckhard Gerdes
WEIRDLY OUT WEST Rhys Hughes
THE POPE'S MUSTARD-MAKER Alfred Jarry
PATENTS PENDING Derek Pell & Doug Skinner
THE UNKNOWN ADJECTIVE & OTHER STORIES Doug Skinner
SLEEPYTIME CEMETERY: 40 STORIES Doug Skinner
CRITICS & MY TALKING DOG Stefan Themerson
TOURIST: A NOVEL Temenuga Trifonova
THE NEW URGE READER 4 Various
101 CARTOONS FROM *LE CHAT NOIR* Various
LE SCAT NOIR ENCYCLOPÉDIE Various
LE SCAT NOIR BEDSIDE NONSENSE Various
THE BEST OF LE SCAT NOIR Various
OULIPO PORNOBONGO ANTHOLOGY Various
APRIL FIREBALL: EARLY STORIES Tom Whalen
CURIOUS IMPOSSIBILITIES Carla M. Wilson
THREE PLAYS BY D. HARLAN WILSON
VAHAZAR Witkacy

Printed in Great Britain
by Amazon